WHISKY WARS OF THE CANADIAN WEST

Fifty Years of Battles Against the Bottle

RICH MOLE

VICTORIA · VANCOUVER · CALGARY

Heritage House Publishing Company Ltd.
heritagehouse.ca

Library and Archives Canada Cataloguing in Publication
Mole, Rich, 1946–
    Whisky wars of the Canadian West: fifty years of battles against the bottle / Rich Mole.

(Amazing stories)
Includes bibliographical references and index.
Issued also in electronic format.
ISBN 978-1-926613-93-2

    1. Temperance—Canada, Western—History. 2. Prohibition—Canada, Western—History. 3. Canada, Western—Social conditions. 4. Canada, Western—Biography. I. Title. II. Series: Amazing stories (Victoria, B.C.)

HV5306.M64 2012   363.4'109712   C2012-901010-3

Series editor: Lesley Reynolds
Proofreader: Liesbeth Leatherbarrow

Cover photo: An illicit still seized by the Alberta Provincial Police near Cardston, Alberta, in the early 1920s. Glenbow Archives NA-2899-13

The interior of this book was produced on 100% post-consumer recycled paper, processed chlorine free and printed with vegetable-based inks.

Heritage House acknowledges the financial support for its publishing program from the Government of Canada through the Canada Book Fund (CBF), Canada Council for the Arts and the province of British Columbia through the British Columbia Arts Council and the Book Publishing Tax Credit.

16 15 14 13 12   1 2 3 4 5
Printed in Canada

Contents

Eye Opener publisher Bob Edwards. Hopeful at the beginning of prohibition, the alcoholic Edwards was disillusioned by the time it ended. GLENBOW ARCHIVES NA-937-12

Prologue

GEORGE HAMMOND WAS LIVID. *The day before, the bluster-ing North-West Territories whisky trader had been forced to buy back his horse from an Assiniboine thief. The price was steep: two kegs of whisky, a blanket and some tobacco. Now, just after dawn, Hammond discovered his horse was missing again. The bellicose trader stomped through Abe Farwell's whisky post, eager to vent his spleen. It helped to have a sympathetic audience, and this morning fate had provided him with one.*

A few yards away, over a dozen wolf trappers calling themselves the Spitzee Cavalry were lounging around their campfires, drinking. They had just spent a dispiriting week riding 125 miles north from the Missouri riverfront hamlet of

Fort Benton, Montana Territory, and Hammond knew why. Like him, these wolfers were victims of horse thieves.

Spitzee leader Tom Hardwick had been outraged to discover that the theft of 40 horses was a low priority for officers of the Second Cavalry housed in Benton's deteriorating fur-trade post. Worse, fellow wolfers taunted them for allowing Cree to steal the mounts right under their noses. Hardwick and co-leader "Captain" John Evans decided to hunt the thieves themselves. Crossing the border and climbing into the Cypress Hills, the Spitzees were short on food and whisky and long on frustration. Farwell supplied them with food and drink to ease their physical needs, but what he had to say only fanned their anger. Neither he nor Moses Solomon, who operated a Battle Creek post opposite Farwell's, had seen any sign of Cree running a herd of 40 horses.

"Goddamn thieving bastards!" Hammond stormed. The trader announced he was ready to "clean out" the nearby Assiniboine camp. The wolfers lifted their booze-bleared eyes. That sounded good to them. They staggered to their feet, loaded their Henry rifles, cinched up revolver-heavy holsters and stumbled out of the fort after Hammond, oblivious to the trader's "stolen" horse, which stood placidly cropping grass nearby.

Chief Little Soldier had been uneasy for days; his camp was too close to the whites. The whisky of nearby traders was proving almost as deadly to his people as smallpox had been. Most of the 250 emaciated Assiniboine crowded into dozens *of lodges had wandered 200 miles in a fruitless search for buffalo. So when Little Soldier told his people they should break camp and move, his exhausted, famished warriors resisted. Now—bellies full of rotgut—many of them were too drunk to do anything. Before long, even the apprehensive chief had collapsed in alcoholic oblivion.*

Hammond strode past the sprawling Assiniboine and grabbed the first two horses he saw. The few warriors still on their feet began to yell. Hammond yelled back. Down in the shelter of a nearby coulee, the Spitzees watching the spectacle saw Hammond stomp back empty-handed. By this time, Abe Farwell was in the coulee too, attempting to convince Hardwick and Evans to avoid trouble; he would bring an interpreter from the fort to help the two sides talk. A shot rang out, then a second. Farwell pleaded for sanity.

Hardwick brushed him off. "We've started in," he sneered, "and we'll clean all of them out, if we can!" As fire erupted all about, Farwell realized some of it was coming from behind him. Traders arrayed on his palisades were also shooting down into the Assiniboine camp.

It took sober, steady hands for the Natives to load, aim and fire 20-year-old muskets faster than once a minute. Sobriety didn't matter to the wolfers: their brass-fitted .44 calibre Henry repeating rifles fired 28 rounds in 60 seconds. The wolfers decimated the wailing women, screaming children and shouting warriors darting around their lodges. The Assiniboine's three suicidal charges against the coulee made the slaughter complete; heaps of bodies grew in front of the wolfers' smoking rifle barrels.

"I will die here," Little Soldier shouted to his wife, resisting as she tried desperately to pull him into hiding. It was a self-fulfilling prophesy. When the shooting and burning were done, the camp lay in smouldering ruins, and Little Soldier lay dead, shot in the chest. His wife and three other captured women were assaulted repeatedly throughout the night.

It was too much for Solomon, Farwell and his Crow wife, Big Mary. The operators torched their palisades and log-and-mud buildings. Along with a number of tent-traders and an Assiniboine woman Big Mary had rescued at gunpoint from the Spitzees, they fled the area.

The Americans hailed the returning wolfers as conquering heroes. The Helena Herald crowed, "Forty Lodges Wiped Out by Sixteen 'Kit Carsons.'" Months later, when news of the massacre reached Ottawa, Canadians simply regarded these "Kit Carsons" as drunken Yankee murderers.

1

Canada Marches Off to War

WORRIED NORTHWEST MISSIONARIES had warned Prime Minister John A. Macdonald that "wholesale poisoning" of Natives by whisky traders would likely lead to tragedy. Macdonald needed a dispassionate view of northwest conditions, so in August 1872, he sent militia colonel Patrick Robertson-Ross west on a fact-finding mission. One month and 1,200 miles later, Robertson-Ross presented his facts personally to Macdonald. Among his findings: during the previous year, 88 Blackfoot had been killed in a series of drunken brawls, and Americans were selling whisky openly to the Natives as far north as Fort Edmonton. The Colonel quoted them as saying that since "there was no force present to prevent them [from doing so], they would do just as they pleased." His report also mentioned whisky posts operating on Dominion soil just north of Fort Benton, Montana Territory, including a major post with the amusing frontier name of Fort Whoop-Up.

Canada Declares War on Whisky

Robertson-Ross's report made important recommendations about stopping the whisky traders. The colonel counselled the prime minister to send a regiment of 550 armed, mounted men into the territories, station them in Hudson's Bay Company (HBC) forts and build another post near the border to thwart American whisky runners. As for uniforms, Robertson-Ross suggested scarlet tunics. Hadn't the Natives around Fort Garry scoffed at the green-coated garrison troops? "We know," they said, "that the soldiers of our Great White Mother wear red coats and are our friends."

Not all of Robertson-Ross's suggestions were new; Macdonald had heard some of them three years before, when Captain William Butler ventured west on behalf of the Lieutenant-Governor of the new "postage-stamp" province of Manitoba. However, Robertson-Ross was the federal government's man and his report was up-to-date. That made all the difference.

A bill to create a mounted police force soon received royal assent. "Police," Macdonald emphasized, not "troops"; no point in ruffling the feathers of American political hawks. But political realities soon intervened. Consumed with the seemingly impossible task of constructing a railroad 1,000 miles longer than the one just completed in the United States and beset with bribery allegations that newspapers were calling the Pacific Scandal, Macdonald had little time or energy for his police force.

However, the tragedy that many had feared had now occurred—even if it had been perpetrated by wolfers, not whisky traders. Many Assiniboine men, women and children had been slaughtered. One hundred? Two hundred? No one was sure of the number. In Ottawa, what mattered more than the number of violent deaths was the fact that the Natives had died at the hands of Americans on Dominion soil. Despite official recognition of Canada's nationhood by the United States, American interlopers might pose a threat to Canadian sovereignty in the West, as the messianic Metis Louis Riel had done as leader of the Red River Rebellion.

Just over four months after the wolfers had laid down their withering fire, the first hastily recruited North West Mounted Police (NWMP) constables were on their way west to Lower Fort Garry. The Assiniboine, it seemed, had not died in vain. Nine months later, on July 8, 1874, fronting a rattling, clanking column that stretched back more than three and a half miles, Colonel George A. French led 274 men of Canada's new "army" away from Dufferin, Manitoba, and out onto what Captain William Butler had called "The Great Lone Land."

In one of Canada's supreme historical ironies, the

commander-in-chief of the Dominion's tiny whisky-war army—the prime minister himself—was a weary, life-long combatant in his own personal war with alcohol. Macdonald's battles with his implacable foe were well known in Ottawa, and many sympathized with the private and public struggles of this gaunt, disappointed, over-worked man. "Indisposed" was the polite term for the prime minister's condition, but everyone knew what the word signified. Those who came in contact with the prime minister met a staggering drunk. In 1873, Macdonald's railroad dream was fading in the dismal dawn of fiscal and political realities. In despair, he proposed his own resignation.

The Whisky Trade

Long before the massacre, the wolfers had become a common enemy of northwest tribes. The trappers baited animal carcasses with strychnine, which not only killed the wolves that bore the fashionable furs, but also the invaluable dogs the Natives used for hunting and packing and as their encampments' early-warning systems. Vengeful Assiniboine, Cree and Blackfoot hunting parties didn't always distinguish between the hated wolfers and any comparatively innocent whites they met. The US 2nd Cavalry hated the wolfers in general, and the odious Spitzees in particular, for making already-inflamed Natives more dangerous. Robust, flint-eyed little John Jerome Healy hated the Spitzees for another reason: they were bad for business. At this particular time in his legendary life, Healy's business was booze.

Travelling west with the US army, Irish-born John Jerome Healy—like tens of thousands of others in the early 1860s—came down with a near-fatal case of gold fever. He headed north to Montana Territory and gold-rich Alder Creek Gulch near burgeoning Virginia City. Restless Healy was soon venturing across the border into Blackfoot Confederacy lands—now Alberta—looking for gold. In 1869, he met Al Hamilton and discovered something more profitable: fur trading. Back in Fort Benton, he mesmerized Hamilton's uncles, merchants Isaac and George Baker, with his trading concept, convincing the pair to stake him and their nephew on a trip back north with trade goods that included whisky. A two- or three-dollar pint purchased a buffalo robe that fetched six dollars in New York. Six months later, when their wagons rolled back into Benton, Healy and Hamilton presented the stunned Bakers with $50,000 worth of furs.

The key to trading success was the whisky. A gallon of genuine, bonded whisky was first watered down to produce four gallons of liquid, then coloured and flavoured with a wide variety of ingredients, from tea, red ink and chewing tobacco to red peppers, ginger and laudanum. Now it was true "Injun Juice." Healy took a perverted pride in concocting a brew that was potentially even more deadly. "I'll fix up 'coffin varnish' so strong," he boasted to Isaac Baker, "you'll be able to shoot an injun through the heart, and he won't die until he's sobered up." It was all legal, too, as the Bakers carefully legitimized liquor transport with Department of Interior "medicinal purposes" permits.

The Natives couldn't get enough of the stuff. Traders reported that chiefs who received a ritual welcome drink at the post asked for a second, knocked it back, but didn't swallow. They hurried outside the gates to spit the booze into the mouths of companions. When they ran out of furs, Natives would trade anything for another bottle, including their lodges, horses and even wives and daughters. As bottles emptied, unbridled orgies ensued.

Why go searching for wandering Natives when you could entice them to come to you? In 1870, the Bakers financed hastily built Fort Hamilton, about 95 miles north of Fort Benton, and placed Healy in charge. When the post burned down, the Bakers hired former HBC master carpenter William Gladstone to construct a replacement. Gladstone took two years and spent $25,000—four times the cost of most posts—but the Bakers never complained. The I.G. Baker Company's investment was a 14-foot-high loopholed stockade of sharpened stakes, stores, warehouses and two corner bastions housing a brass cannon and a small mountain howitzer. Barracks of heavy, squared timbers were topped with earth-covered roofs to protect workers against fire arrows and were finished with iron-barred doors, windows and chimneys to discourage crazed drunks.

The large wicket in the barred, oaken stockade doors guaranteed safe trade exchanges.

Healy was a profit-hungry visionary, but a bad manager, so Isaac Baker installed clever Donald Davis, a larcenous former cavalry bookkeeper, to run the place under Healy's supervision. Competition—most notably T.C. Power and courtly John D. Weatherwax—built their own whisky posts. None of them compared to the new Fort Hamilton, which remained unnamed until a fort freighter pulled up at I.G. Baker's for more whisky and announced that business up north was "Whoopin' them up!" From then on, the biggest whisky post in the Canadian territories was known as Fort Whoop-Up.

Just a few weeks before the Cree ran off the Spitzee horses, wolfers began blackmailing whisky traders, whose stock in trade for furs and buffalo robes included not only bottles of aptly named *Iskotawapoo* ("fire liquid" in Cree) but also repeating rifles. Blackfoot warriors turned those same rifles on wolfers. John Healy was among the first to hear the news that some Spitzee had coerced $1,300 worth of furs out of the manager at Fort Kipp, located northeast of Whoop-Up. Healy guessed spiteful Spitzees would make his post their next target. "Am going to sell to the Indians anything they want to buy," Healy wrote to Hardwick and Evans in Fort Benton. "I will have traders out on the prairie. You may meet some of them. Please do not interfere with them . . . If you have anything to say," Healy concluded haughtily, "come to me, I am the one who is responsible." A boisterous meeting convened by the Spitzee confirmed the success of Healy's wolfer-baiting strategy. Healy hit the Whoop-Up trail. A few days later, he dismissed everyone in the fort except the cook and made secret preparations. He was sitting in a trading room, holding a jar of hooch, when 18 Spitzees rode into the post.

"There's word you're selling guns to the injuns," challenged wolfer Harry "Kamoose" ("Squaw Thief") Taylor. Healy defused the challenge with beguiling Whoop-Up hospitality, ordering the cook to sizzle some buffalo steaks for the tired riders. After dinner and drinks, Healy led them all back to the trading room, sat comfortably behind the counter and nonchalantly lit up an oversized cigar. The Spitzees decided to get down to business. Taylor repeated his charge. Healy, stroking his impeccably trimmed goatee, seemed oblivious.

"Well, what do you say about it?" demanded John Evans.

"Guilty! And you be damned!" Healy roared. "What right have you to come down here and try *me*," he railed, pointing at Taylor, "a renegade from justice?" (Native justice, at least, since the woman Taylor had stolen was the daughter of a Blackfoot chief.) Healy thrust his cigar at others in turn. "You! You! You're mad dogs!" The defiant wolfers levelled revolvers and rifles, and one took a few menacing steps toward the counter. Healy pulled a sawed-off shotgun from a shelf near his chair and thumped it on the countertop, then yanked a concealing blanket off the fort's small mountain howitzer, its muzzle pointed straight at Whoop-Up's visitors. Healy puffed on his cigar until the tip was red-hot and held it over the howitzer's touch hole.

"If you move a hand or take another step towards me," Healy warned, "I'll blow you all to hell! Now git!" The Spitzee backed out of the room and dashed to their horses, chased by Healy's hectoring taunts. "Eighteen to one!" he laughed, following them out into the night, shotgun hammer cocked. "Next time, you'd better bring forty!"

A few months later, watching the cheering throngs welcome the Spitzee back from their Cypress Hills killing spree, Healy likely wasn't surprised to hear George Hammond was the instigator. Years before, Hammond had shown up at Whoop-Up with a bunch of traders intent on wiping out a band of murderous Indians. (It was accepted wisdom at the time that white men were never murderous, only Indians were; adopted by white men, the same tactics were seen as brilliant or inspired.) To do the job, they wanted to buy ammunition—on credit. Not only did this bunch want to kill his customers, Healy shrewdly figured them for a bad credit risk. When Healy refused them, Hammond turned surly. Healy took his fists and feet to the blustering bully and threw him out of the fort.

It was obvious to Healy and his boss, Isaac Baker, that wolfers were jeopardizing the whisky trade. Perhaps it was time for a career change—maybe become a newspaper editor to champion the cause. At least he would be out of harm's way if trouble came. When trouble eventually did come, Healy could not have imagined it would roll down the streets of Fort Benton in broad daylight.

Engaging the Enemy

On September 24, 1874, something resembling a unit of the British Army clattered into town. Although their white helmets and pill-box hats were besmudged and battered and their red tunics tattered—they had obviously been on the trail for months—the travel-worn group still managed to look faintly military. Baker and Healy knew where the strangers had come from. Methodist John McDougall, who had just built a mission in the midst of the Mountain Stoneys (near today's Banff), had given Healy the news of the unit's formation himself, during a visit to Whoop-Up. Weeks before, when police reached Blackfoot country, a man named Jerry Potts knew of their arrival, and before long, the Bakers knew too. They also knew that the force had been sent to put them out of the whisky trade. Well, the pragmatic Bakers likely concluded, so be it. The buffalo and the profitable hide trade were disappearing fast, and so were the traders' customers, killed off by starvation, rifle-fire and the traders' own deadly liquid merchandise.

After Commissioner George French and Assistant Commissioner James Macleod walked into the telegraph office to wire Ottawa, Isaac Baker gave them a short, fulsome, streetside speech of welcome and offered the officers his fashionable home as overnight respite from wilderness rigours. After a sumptuous dinner, Baker eagerly assured Macleod that he could provide everything on the colonel's long list of provisions. Over brandy and cigars, Baker asked French how he could help the police in their mission to stamp out the whisky trade. The policemen suggested he help them find Fort Whoop-Up. Baker told them that the scout Bear Child, who called himself Jerry Potts, was certain to know Whoop-Up's whereabouts. Baker was also certain he had plenty of time to tell Healy to get wagons rattling up the trail to empty the post.

Guided by the astonishing Potts, who had a Blood mother and a Scottish father, 150 policemen under James Macleod moved north toward Whoop-Up. Potts knew everything about the wilderness it seemed; he killed and dressed a buffalo cow for the column's lunch and found the sweetest, clearest water the men had swallowed in weeks. Days later, after climbing a rise, the men gazed down at the eerily quiet post. Field guns and mortars were quickly unlimbered and trained on the stockade, and men took up siege positions. Macleod shouted down to the post. There was no answer. Potts began to amble down to the fort, and Macleod jumped in the saddle and followed.

The two dismounted in front of the gate, and Potts thudded the stock of his Henry on its timbers. A lone American named Dave Akers swung the gate open. Akers claimed he owned the post; the manager and others were "away on business." A search found little evidence of whisky, although in certain places the men could smell it strongly enough. Macleod was deeply suspicious, but what could he prove? Akers invited Macleod to dinner. Nonplussed, Macleod accepted the invitation and dismissed the men. The NWMP hadn't really "taken" the northwest's most notorious whisky post; the whisky traders had simply given it to them. Nevertheless, Colonel Macleod let Akers and his right-hand man know exactly where they stood. "From this day on I'm the law out here and I'll arrest anyone I even *think* is trading whisky," he warned. "I've got the authority to try any man and with a wink from Ottawa, I'll hang him!"

Macleod was impressed with Whoop-Up's formidable structure. Winter was coming; the men would need a fort of their own, and here was one ready-made. Before the meal of roast buffalo, garden vegetables and canned peaches was finished, Macleod offered Akers $10,000 for the fort. Akers countered with $25,000. Too much, Macleod thought. A few days later, Potts led the police to a cottonwood grove on the Oldman River about 100 miles northwest, the site of the future Fort Macleod. How fortunate that Isaac Baker employed men familiar with fort construction! Site activity was supervised by Donald Davis, former Whoop-Up manager. Building items were laboriously freighted up by Baker's long bull trains—oxen straining in harness, bull-whackers cursing and shouting—exactly as Whoop-Up's whisky and supplies had been delivered a few weeks before.

Fort Macleod was still under construction when a minor chief rode in to tell Macleod that William Bond, a black man, had traded him liquor for two ponies. Guided by Potts, 10 Mounties saddled up to investigate. Two days later, they were back, driving two confiscated wagons full of whisky, rifles, revolvers and a pile of buffalo robes and with Bond, Taylor and three other traders in custody. The traders were each fined as much as $200, a significant sum in 1874. None could pay. "Waxy" Weatherwax finally appeared to pay fines and arrange releases for all except Bond, likely deciding he could fend for himself. (He fended admirably: while being transferred from one building to another, Bond made a dash for freedom, escaping unscathed in spite of a quick-witted sentry's rifle fire.)

Weatherwax did not fare so well. In February 1875, Sub-Inspector Cecil Denny led a patrol through the snow to the foot of the Rockies. After dumping a five-gallon container of whisky, they persuaded Peigan villagers to guide them to the traders' camp. There, 10 gallons of "bug juice" were destroyed and 200 buffalo robes confiscated. The Mounties followed the trail of the fleeing trader to a cabin. Inside, three card-playing traders, including Weatherwax, were taken by surprise and arrested. Denny and his men rounded up the horses, loaded hundreds of robes aboard the traders' sleighs and poured the whisky onto the snow.

"Feeling quite pleased with our success," as Denny recalled, the Mounties and their prisoners made for Fort Macleod.

Unable to pay their $250 fines, two traders were tossed into the guardhouse. Belligerent Weatherwax threatened to wire Washington, DC, over this outrageous treatment of American citizens. Macleod was unimpressed—the nearest telegrapher's key was back in Benton, and the prisoner obviously wasn't going to go anywhere—so Waxy could work off his fine by mucking stables and cutting wood. "We had no idea that the persons or property of American citizens would be trifled with," grumbled editor John Healy in the *Fort Benton Record*, perhaps still bitter over lost whisky-trade revenue.

In 1875, the US Cavalry arrested Tom Hardwick, John Evans and five others implicated in the Cypress Hills massacre. Ottawa wanted them extradited, but amid noisy demonstrations in Helena, where their trials were held, all were set free and lauded in a torchlight parade. Upon their arrival in Fort Benton, a holiday was declared. John Evans decided to open a saloon and named it "Extradition."

Just one year after the NWMP marched west, whisky traders had ceased to be a threat. Years later, John Healy had some sardonic words about that: "If we had only been allowed to carry on the business in our own way for another two years there would have been no trouble . . . whisky, pistols, strychnine and other like processes would have effectively cleared away these wretched natives."

Unlike the experience on the American frontier, in which lawmen were late arrivals, the mounted police had arrived on the Canadian prairie before settlers, towns or the railroad, a wonderful set of circumstances for Benton businessmen. Working just across the border, the reformed whisky-war troops of generals T.C. Power and Isaac and George Baker would never again duck arrows or dodge bullets.

Two other NWMP posts quickly followed the first. In May, Jerry Potts led B Division to the site of the outbreak of "war," the Cypress Hills. There, not far from the scene of the massacre, police built a fort named after their leader, Inspector James Walsh. In late summer, just north of Fort Macleod, I.G. Baker's construction crews built Fort Calgary. Around each post, a little cluster of businesses opened, including T.C. Power and Baker stores and billiard halls. At Fort Macleod, William Gladstone, the man who built Whoop-Up, operated a carpentry shop, and by 1880, the little town boasted one of the few hotels in the territory; the owner was none other than Harry "Kamoose" Taylor.

Some years later, Waxy Weatherwax became a liquor wholesaler in Fort Benton. When Inspector Cecil Denny and others dropped in to say hello, Weatherwax "bore us no grudge, and seemed glad to see us," Denny remembered. Knowing full well the effect of whisky "upon the red men," and even when he knew traders "shamefully abused the men and debauched the women," Denny nevertheless was of the opinion that "these whisky traders . . . with few exceptions, were not a bad lot, and many, in time, became good law-abiding citizens."

CHAPTER

The Law They Couldn't Enforce

IN LATE 1885, WHEN THE MOUNTIES arrived at the premises of Calgary councillor Simon J. Clarke to search for whisky, things did not go as planned—for the police, Clarke or indeed, the town. This member of Calgary's inner circle immediately made his contempt for the redcoats clear by grabbing one constable by the shoulder and threatening him with an empty bottle. Shouting and gesturing, Clarke managed to hold two other officers at bay for 10 minutes—time enough, it seems, for bottles to be safely carried out of the law's reach. So instead of charging him with violating the liquor laws of the revised North-West Territories Act, the police settled for charges of resisting arrest and assault.

A Wide-Open Town

Four days later, Clarke's supporters, the railway shanty-town's movers and shakers, filled Judge Jeremiah Travis's courtroom. To Mayor George Murdoch, solicitor and councillor Henry Bleeker and Chief of Police J.S. Ingram, importing and selling liquor in this brutally harsh, numbingly monotonous place and time was regarded more an act of charity than a crime. Liquor provided a blissful escape from frontier discomfort and tedium. Besides, who could blame an individual for using his civic connections to pursue an entrepreneurial sideline?

Alas for Clarke and his lawyer, E.P. Davis, teetotaler Judge Jeremiah Travis was in no mood to be lenient. In his summation, he announced he had seen two drunks on the street himself (on a recent Sunday, no less!), and a woman battered at the hands of her drunken spouse had come to him pleading for redress. Gaunt, forbidding Travis glared over at the prisoner and sentenced the civic leader to six months at hard labour.

Travis's sentence undoubtedly pleased those at the new police barracks, and it should have pleased the tiny town's civic leaders, too. After all, the same mayor and council had originally pressured the Regina-based North-West Territories Council to appoint a legitimate stipendiary magistrate, arguing that no individual could expect dispassionate justice when tried by officers of arresting constables. It was one thing, their petition inferred, for police to enforce the law (although conducting searches without warrants was another bone of contention), but it was intolerable to have senior officers such as Inspector Sam Steele serving as both judge and jury.

Their concerns about due process seem laudable. However, these were men who placed profits before principles. The not-so-secret motivation for their outrage was the fact that the NWMP was bad for business. The business of early-1880s Calgary was putting money in the town's coffers. When a violent drunk was arrested by one of Ingram's town cops for disturbing the peace, his resulting fine went straight into the hands of Calgary treasurer Charles Sparrow. However, if a Calgarian was arrested by the Mounties for the territorial offence of illegal possession of alcohol, his fine was locked in a railcar safe and rolled off to Ottawa. At one point, the incensed mayor wrote Ottawa demanding the Mounties stay out of town.

Chief Ingram was very knowledgeable about crime, simply because he was a thug. Kicked out of the Winnipeg police for beating up one of his own constables, then punching out a resident for driving his buggy too fast, Ingram was also identified as a customer in a house of ill-repute. The year before Mayor Murdoch hired him as police chief, Ingram, now a gambler, was again charged with assault.

Travis understood all this and more. Both the mayor and lawyer E.P. Davis had been seen staggering from a brothel. However, prostitution provided more than recreation.

Members of Calgary's first town council—and whisky ring—assembled in a composite photograph. Front row, extreme left: Mayor George Murdoch. Back row, third from left: solicitor and councillor Henry Bleeker; sixth from left, Simon J. Clarke; seventh from left, Chief J.S. Ingram. GLENBOW ARCHIVES NA-644-30

Madams paid up too, providing a lucrative civic revenue stream. Businessman George Marsh had no doubt about that, and Murdoch himself admitted it when he attempted to persuade Marsh to forget his crusade to close a particular brothel (perhaps the very one he frequented). Madams knew that they might occasionally be arrested but never jailed; a fine would suffice nicely.

Travis was told Ingram had paid a visit to the owner of a new saloon informing him that for a certain fee, he could avoid troublesome police raids. The city council was operating a protection racket! Marsh bent Travis's ear: the mayor, some of his councillors and the police chief were all members of a "whisky ring." Had Travis known about Calgary's bloody, booze-related history, the link between whisky and the town's who's who would not have been surprising.

Back in 1871, flush with Whoop-Up's success, Johnny Healy had convinced former Montana sheriff Fred Kanouse to hit the trail and build a post on the Elbow River, three miles from the site of the future Fort Calgary. During the fort's first trading season, a trader smashed his revolver into the face of a particularly unruly Blood warrior. The Bloods retreated with their bruised comrade. Kanouse sympathized with his trader, but knew violence was bad for business. Fred's decision to ride out with the trader to the Blood camp to smooth things over proved fatal.

The angry Bloods saw the two traders approach, and before Kanouse could utter a word, rifle fire from the camp spun his companion out of his saddle. A bullet tore into Kanouse's arm, just below the shoulder. The trader yanked his horse around and, leaving his dead employee behind, galloped back to the fort with the Bloods in hot pursuit. Kanouse, his wife and traders fought them off for three days, until a Blackfoot was paid to hurry to get help at Fort Spitzee, located west of the future town of High River. Once they saw the rescuers draw near, the Bloods vanished. The Elbow post operated profitably for two more bloody seasons, during which time two horse thieves were shot dead by traders and Blood chief Red Crow killed his own brother in a drunken argument.

Following Healy's lead, trader Dick Berry began to build a post on the Elbow. The Bloods attacked the men while they were still sharpening stakes and sawing logs. Berry moved farther upstream to a new site located within the boundaries of present-day Calgary. Just after the post was finished, Bloods ambushed Berry outside its walls, shot and killed him and ran off the traders' horses. Berry's bunch fled on foot to Kanouse's post, borrowed mounts and galloped south while the Bloods burned their post to the ground.

The height of Calgary craziness took place just a few months before Judge Travis's appointment. By May 1885, the Canadian Militia had beaten Louis Riel and his Metis and Native allies. A few weeks later, Inspector Sam Steele led his "buckskin cavalry," Steele's Scouts, in a Northwest Rebellion victory parade under flags, evergreen archways and signs proclaiming "Calgary welcomes Alberta's heroes." That evening, citizens celebrated so boozily that a dozen hotel operators were arrested for selling whisky. Carousing crowds grew incensed until they realized that the hoteliers would appear before none other than Mayor George Murdoch, leader of the whisky ring, in his other civic role as Justice of the Peace. At this news, anger turned to hilarity.

Judge Travis Bought Off

When the judge's gavel came down on poor Simon Clarke, any smugness citizens might have felt at their success in having a legitimate magistrate appointed to their tiny town evaporated. Two days after Clarke's sentencing, the mayor convened a rowdy "indignation meeting" inside Boynton Hall. After a number of suggestions, including that a barrel of dynamite be placed under Judge Travis to "blow him to hell," protesters agreed on a much less explosive course of action: send a delegation to Ottawa to have Travis's decision overturned.

Travis was infuriated at the news. Fuelling his fury was the discovery of his court clerk, Hugh Cayley, stumbling down a street "stupidly drunk," his duties forgotten. Travis fired the man. Unfortunately, Cayley also had an influential sideline as editor of the new *Calgary Herald*, which began vicious attacks on the judge. Travis charged the editor of the "dirty, slanderous little sheet" with contempt of court. When Cayley refused to pay the fine, Travis threw him in jail. Lawyer E.P. Davis ran the newspaper in Cayley's absence, and the criticisms continued. In addition to his legal practice and temporary stint as editor, Davis was also the chair of the local Liberal Association. He suggested solicitor Henry Bleeker make some discreet long-distance enquiries about how to get rid of Conservative appointee Travis. An Ottawa Liberal lawyer suggested a "newspaper war" might prove beneficial. Soon, the Liberal-leaning *Manitoba Free Press* and *Toronto Globe* began running letters critical of Travis's high-handed actions. In far-off Saint John, New Brunswick, the editor of the *Daily Sun* sadly suggested that "the abstract sense of justice which seems to influence Judge Travis has led him astray."

In court, Travis exposed Murdoch's involvement with whisky merchants and made the stunning allegation that E.P. Davis was, in fact, no lawyer at all—he had never passed his bar exams. Travis banned Davis from his courtroom for two years. As a civic election loomed, Travis alleged that voters lists stacked with Murdoch supporters were fraudulent and barred the mayor and councillors from holding office for two years. Nevertheless, their names still appeared on ballots, and they won. Travis disqualified them, which left nobody in a position to run the town.

Despite the fact that Travis had the backing of 85 percent of the town's businessmen, the "Bleeker-Murdoch-Cayley-Davis quartette" (described by Travis to the prime minister as a "drunken utterly worthless set") eventually won the day. With the Northwest Rebellion put down and the railway finally finished, the exhausted federal Conservative government had no stomach for another battle. It simply reorganized the territory's courts and chose not to offer Travis a position. The zealous law-and-order advocate was encouraged to return to private practice. It's easy to see Travis as a casualty of friendly fire in Canada's whisky wars. However, as an inducement to leave the field, as it were, the government endowed him with a generous lifetime annual pension.

The Territorial Laughingstocks

NWMP Great March veterans such as Inspector Sam Steele could be forgiven for being a little wistful about "the good old days," when it had been easy to confiscate furs, pour out whisky and fine or jail the traders. However, once Canadian Pacific's rails were down and its stations up, settlers arrived. Many were Europeans, and liquor was part of their culture, society and religion. Decent, law-abiding men took a drink, more often than not home-brewed, and broke the law, a law the inspector himself called "an insult to a free people." Steele scoffed, "The prohibitory law made more drunkards than if there had been an open bar and free drinks on every street corner. The officers and men hated the detestable [prohibition] duty."

Enforcement difficulties forced the government to revise the North-West Territories Act. Permits made liquor importation and its possession for personal use legal. The revision made a bad situation worse. Hotel and saloon owners quickly began using the "personal use" permits to sell whisky to the public, as Calgary alderman Clarke probably had done. The permit holder could give his permit to anyone at any time. Permits were neither dated nor stamped and thus remained valid long after a particular permitted bottle was emptied. The bottle was refilled again and again, sometimes with cheaper spirits supplied by American rum-runners who had eluded NWMP border patrols. By 1887, Commissioner Lawrence Herchmer commented that it was "really curious the extraordinary length of time some holders of permits can keep their liquor." Railroad trains made liquor smuggling easier than ever, and police found whisky hidden everywhere, in pseudo-books, oyster cans, sardine tins, coal-oil cans and barrels and luggage trunks. Herchmer made his feelings clear: "The permit system should be done away with in the first place if the law is to be enforced."

Superintendent J.H. McIllree, who found many of the permit stubs held by Calgary hotel- and saloon-keepers made out to men who had left the country or were already dead, stated the obvious: "Of course, everyone knows whisky is sold in nearly every saloon in Calgary." If McIllree's men were lucky enough to make an arrest and confiscation, it remained almost impossible for police to get a conviction. Worse, wrote McIllree, "My men, endeavouring to do their duty, are made a laughing stock of."

Saloons and bars legally sold a 4 percent "mild" hop beer, which was judged to be non-intoxicating. The police were now burdened with investigating breweries to ensure that the legal limit of alcohol was not exceeded. Even when Macleod constables got drunk on the stuff, their commanding officer was unable to prove alcohol-content infractions.

Frustrated constables secretly sympathized with the men they were arresting. Once out of uniform, there wasn't much to distinguish them from their prisoners. When not fighting fires, chasing horse thieves, wrestling lunatics and breaking up fights, the young policemen were bored and restless, especially when winter claustrophobia set it. The policemen were as susceptible to the lure of liquor as anyone else. When H troop finally got its back pay, their prolonged binge terrorized the town of Lethbridge. In Saskatoon, a couple of tipsy Mounties held up a pedestrian on Main Street, lifted his wallet and continued their spree at their victim's expense. At Fort Macleod, citizens ducked for cover when drunken policemen let loose with their revolvers. "This blazing away with a pistol whenever a man gets drunk, whether it be in the hands of a policeman or a civilian is getting monotonous," the *Macleod Gazette* grumbled, "and must be put down."

If he couldn't stop his men from drinking, Herchmer decided, he could at least control the imbibing. He established a police canteen on the base in Regina in 1881. One hundred gallons of 4 percent legal beer was brought in every week. A glass of beer cost a man less than half of what he paid in hotel bars. Almost immediately, Regina's Board of Trade condemned Herchmer's innovation as detrimental to business. Nevertheless, within a year, NWMP canteens were also operating in Fort Calgary, Fort Macleod and at Lethbridge, where they succeeded in raising the holy hackles of churchmen. The Presbyterian Synod of Canada passed a convention resolution calling for an end to police canteens. When the ministers were advised that canteens sold only beer and that they stopped men from buying stronger drink in towns, the resolution was filed away and forgotten. It was as close to a victory in the never-ending war on whisky as the Mounties were likely to enjoy, and a fleeting one at that.

By the time this photo was taken inside Fort Macleod around 1911, public displays of Mountie drunkenness were just a bad memory. On the table are mugs of temperance beer—the only beverage sold in Commissioner Herchmer's post canteens. GLENBOW ARCHIVES PA-3481-5

After almost two decades of pleading for changes to the liquor laws, the police finally got what they wanted. In 1891, the permit system was suspended and liquor enforcement turned over to the North-West Territories Council. The following year, the council licensed saloons and hired inspectors to enforce closing laws and other regulations. Mounties heaved a collective sigh of relief. Unless liquor infractions involved criminal activity, such as assault or robbery, the Mounties were no longer involved.

By the turn of the century, the NWMP was griping again; the new licensing system wasn't working. Drinking continued, especially after autumn harvests put more money in men's pockets. Overworked and underpaid town cops with better things to do ignored inebriated combatants, confident that bellicose drunks tossed out of saloons would simply stumble off into an alley to sleep their way to short-term sobriety. "The prevailing idea . . . that the law regulates the sale of liquor and tends to the decrease of drunkenness is farcical to the last degree," snorted Regina NWMP inspector Charles Constantine. As soon as a liquor inspector turned his back, Constantine confessed, "Wholesale drunkenness goes on." Drunkenness was nothing new, even in Winnipeg, that centre of prairie urbanity.

By the 1890s, "wholesale drunkenness" had been a fact of Winnipeg life for at least a decade. "The worst place for drinking I ever saw!" a visitor making his way west had scrawled in an 1883 diary entry. Being from Chicago—a metropolis 30 times the size of Manitoba's capital—the former harness-maker was a good judge of the situation. His observation sounds like a criticism, but it wasn't. That westward traveller quickly realized the business implications of Canadians' prodigious thirsts. Thousands of others had taken advantage of it, and that traveller, George Murdoch, would soon do the same, as the leader of Calgary's whisky ring.

3

The Booze Capital of Western Canada

IT WAS A WINNIPEG PAYDAY. That winter afternoon, as men streamed out of railyards, warehouses, packing plants and offices, most did not head home. Like humble office clerk Harry Gray, they headed straight to hotels, where barkeeps happily accepted their cheques and filled their glasses. Hours later, befuddled Harry stumbled out of a bar into a snow-covered alley somewhere between the Clarendon and Queen's Hotels. Vague silhouettes—three or four, Harry couldn't remember—moved in quickly. Shoves became punches, and once Harry fell, punches turned to kicks. "Robbed of what was left of his pay," his son James Gray recalled decades later, Harry was "left to die in the snow."

"Rolling drunks" represented easy money in Winnipeg.

It was especially easy that winter night in 1913. Harry Gray could not have fought off his attackers even if he had been stone sober. Harry had only one arm.

A City of Payday Drunks

Winnipeg had always been a jumping-off place for those seeking the adventure, opportunity or simply the anonymity offered by the North-West Territories. When Canadian Pacific (CP) locomotives replaced Red River carts, the far reaches of the Canadian west were suddenly within easy reach of Ontario and the eastern US. Winnipeg's resulting growth was stunning. The hamlet of 5,000 souls in 1875 became a city of 16,000 citizens by the end of 1882. The new, easy territorial access also meant there was a premium on sleeping space for travellers. Soon, thousands of tradesmen and carpenters were on their way from points east, lured by would-be hoteliers' promises of up to five dollars a day. By 1882, there were 86 operating hotels. The real revenue wasn't made through booking second- and third-storey rooms, however; it was made pouring drinks inside street-level bars.

Like smaller towns farther west, 1880s Winnipeg was almost devoid of leisure or recreational facilities. There were no swimming pools or libraries, few edifying classes or workshops. There were only bars and saloons, malodorous, smoke-filled rooms in which the only furniture was likely to be a row of brass spittoons dripping expectorated tobacco juice. Unwashed men simply stood at the bar—or in long queues waiting to reach it—and drank. There was yet another type of place to buy and even consume whisky and rum, just a few feet away from rows of canned goods and sacks of flour and beans. In 1882, there were 64 Winnipeg food stores selling booze by the bottle and offering something the bars and saloons didn't: a place to sit down to drink it, even if the "chair" was only a merchandise barrel.

The measure of a man in this macho 19th-century society was his willingness to "treat." Every man was expected to buy a round for his buddies. Men's pay soon vanished with their sobriety. As James Gray later recounted, "By eight [o'clock] the good natured jostling around the bar would have given way to petulant pushing and the first of the evening's brawls would have brought the first bodily ejections into the street."

By the time Harry, his pregnant wife Maria and six-year-old Jimmie moved to Winnipeg from rural Manitoba in 1911, boom times were back, spawned by astonishingly successful immigration campaigns. The Dominion government persuaded millions to journey thousands of miles to the Canadian prairies, and many stepped through the grand portico of Winnipeg station. The Grays' journey was much shorter, but they were among the last of an influx into a city that grew from 40,000 to 200,000 between the late 1890s and the eve of the First World War.

The railway-era building boom was a distant memory, but its hotel culture was still part of the city's way of life. Although the original clapboard hotel shanties had become

Main Street, Winnipeg, in 1882. When the photographer uncovered his lens for this shot, the city of 16,000 people boasted 86 hotels— most housing saloons. GLENBOW ARCHIVES NA-118-23

imposing two- and three-storey brick buildings, inside dozens of hotel saloons and bars, men were still quickly knocking back as much whisky and beer as they could hold. Citizens' casual habit of stepping over or around comatose drunks hadn't changed either. It took an independent, even austere man to avoid liquor's social pressures. Thin, short, handicapped Harry Gray was not that man.

The One-Armed Man's Battle with the Bottle

Railway worker Gray, who never earned more than $60 a month during the first six years of his marriage, had managed to save $2,000 by the time he packed up his family for

Winnipeg. Just over a year later, Harry had drunk away the nest egg and the family was living with relatives. Even the horrific experience of being beaten almost to death and the resulting five-week hospital recuperation from double pneumonia could not stop Harry's habitual payday rendezvous at the hotel saloons on Main, Market or Queen's Streets.

Harry's wife and brothers wracked their brains—and blasted Harry's ears—about the cause of his destructive habit. Was it the loss of his arm, mangled by a train and amputated years before Harry met Maria? Possibly. Was it because his handicap cost him his chosen sales career and destroyed his self-respect? Perhaps. Well, so what? Jimmie's uncles argued, others had lost limbs and hadn't let that ruin their lives. "Go into a bar on your way home and have a drink or glass of beer or two and then leave!" Harry's brothers shouted. "Why do you always have to make a pig of yourself and not stop till you've drunk yourself out of house and home?"

"I just don't know," Harry would mumble. "I try. God knows I try. But I don't know what happens to me. I just don't know."

On occasions such as this, Jimmie looked for a chance to escape. With his little brother in tow, he would slip away from the family row, a confrontation that "we never understood and . . . always seemed to end with my mother in tears."

As a mature man, James Gray came to understand and admit much more. Far from being a jolly tippler, his father was a "violent drunk and a wife beater, given to vomiting on his clothes and messing his pants," one who routinely pilfered the paper-route money Jimmie and his brother saved to give to their mother for food, the nickels and dimes squandered, instead, on whisky. There were afternoons when Jimmie would hunch over pen and paper, composing pleading letters from mother to uncles, begging for rent money. As painful as these wounds were, they were at least suffered in private. The public hurts exacted a far more excruciating pain.

"Jimmie," his anxious mother would ask, at the end of a payday afternoon, "run down to the corner and see if you can see Daddy. He may have fallen and hurt himself." Sometimes he had. Sometimes Harry hadn't even left the bar.

"Harry, get that God-damn kid the hell out of here!" Gray recalled the Queen's Hotel barkeep shouting when he saw Jimmie standing in the midst of the crowded saloon. "You want me fired and lose the hotel its licence?" Jimmie usually retreated to the lobby to wait for his father, but on one occasion, he didn't budge, except to dodge the punch his dad threw at him. Finally, the boy would lead the man away, praying he wouldn't meet any of his school pals. In summer, when kids played outdoors, God didn't listen.

"Hey, there's Jimmie Gray, taking his old man home again," some chum would yell. Stumbling past, "with my father staggering and leaning on me," Jimmie would hide his face and pretend he didn't hear.

Bailiffs called with eviction notices. "If they were kindly bailiffs, they would stack [personal effects] on the veranda while we searched for alternative accommodation," Gray recalled. If they were not kindly, the bailiffs would dump the Grays' possessions onto the sidewalk. It was Jimmie's humiliating duty, on those bitter winter days, to sit on the curb guarding what was left of the family's possessions as his parents searched out another landlord kind-hearted enough to take them in.

Like almost every other schoolboy in the city, Jimmie worked at a succession of part-time jobs, delivering fish and chips, groceries, photo engravings and messages at the Winnipeg Grain Exchange. In a ring between the barns at River Park, he earned money as a "hot walker," cooling off overheated thoroughbreds between races. He most often handed the money he earned to his mother.

One day, an accidental discovery at the racetrack led to a financial windfall. When not drinking, Winnipeggers were gambling. Thousands stepped up to River Park's newly installed parimutuel wickets. Many bettors were slow learners when it came to understanding the difference between straight, place and show. Many who bet on horses to place or show threw away their tickets when their horse finished first, or straight. Jimmie idly scavenged discarded tickets and compared them with the numbers posted on the results board.

"On that historic afternoon I found and cashed more than fifty dollars worth of winning tickets that the bettors had thrown away in their ignorance," Gray later wrote. That was big money when three pounds of tea sold for just one dollar, $2.50 bought 50 pounds of rice and the price of a

98-pound sack of flour was a mere $2.75. "I went home with money in every pocket and I emptied them one after the other in front of my mother's bulging eyes . . . for we were in a desperate economic downspin at the time, and the money saved our family from imminent disaster."

Harry Gray's inability to provide for his family had a long-term consequence for his oldest son. By 1922, at age 16, Jimmie was dreaming of becoming a civil engineer because they "built great bridges and tunnels and made lots of money." However, his career dream was shattered when his father was fired from his city-hall job for stealing petty cash to buy drinks. Jimmie dropped out to search for full-time work, fated never to be a student again.

The Gray family's sad saga was not unusual; tens of thousands of mothers and children suffered at the hands of drunken husbands and fathers. "Drunkenness was so much a part of ordinary life in Winnipeg, that even the kids I played with took it mostly in their stride," Gray recalled. Youngsters eyed drunks "as a manifestation of life, like dogs that barked at bicycles." As prosperity spurred on by the railroad turned prairie hamlets into towns and cities, the desperate battle against the bottle was fought in uncountable homes.

If families such as the Grays and others on the front line were going to win domestic whisky wars, they needed reinforcements. Before the 20th century dawned, battle lines were drawn between groups named "the wets" and "the drys." The ultimate rallying cry of the drys became "Prohibition!"

CHAPTER

The Drys

BY 1883, BAPTIST MINISTER Reverend A.A. Cameron had seen too many bruised wives and heard too many heart-rending tales from distraught women of empty larders and broken promises (not to mention broken bones). Like other Winnipeg churchmen, frustrated Cameron looked out over his congregation each Sunday and saw very few men. Husbands and fathers were still back home, comatose from Saturday-night carousing. Perhaps, churchmen told each other, they should pressure the city to close the bars earlier on Saturday nights. It was at this point that Reverend Cameron took it upon himself to undertake a course of action that was without precedent. In 21st-century terms, what Cameron set out to do was take a survey. One Saturday night, Cameron laced up his shoes, slapped on his hat and set out to tour Winnipeg's boisterous bars.

Cameron did head counts, guesstimating from 20 to 30 drinkers in each smaller place to over 150 in each of the larger hotel bars. He talked to some of the imbibers. Why, he asked, would they stand around in such smoky, stinking, noisy places? Where else is there to go? drinkers replied. What else is there to do? After visiting just one-third of the city's bars and having already counted roughly 1,000 drinkers, Cameron called it a night. The immediate benefit of his research was a most heartfelt sermon the next Sunday. What the city needed and what the churches must provide, he told his parishioners, were recreational facilities. Yet, years later, after churchmen and city fathers addressed that need, the drinking problem still remained.

Thirty years after Reverend Cameron delivered his sermon's remedy, Maria Gray had her own solution to drunkenness. "Oh, God," her sons heard her wail more than once, "if only we could get rid of those accursed bars!"

Women burdened with drinking husbands knew there was little chance of reforming men who seemed incapable of walking past a bar (especially when their friends were stepping *into* it). The logical alternative was to close them down. There was some evidence to support the notion. Every year, hundreds of farm wives had their once-a-year shopping trips to the big city ruined when their usually sober and hard-working farmer husbands slapped down their money in front of barkeeps instead of spending it inside shops and stores.

Women's banish-the-bar sloganeering caught the sympathetic ears of suffering retailers. Money spent in bars was money that they needed in *their* cash registers. At the height of the 1880s boom, *Winnipeg Times* readers were informed that a dozen butcher shops would no longer do business on credit—too many wives were pleading for meat "on the tab" because their husbands had drunk away family food money. Factory and shop foremen and office managers were also onside. The day after payday, they wanted men on the job, not back home shaking in their sheets with delirium tremens. When the men arrived for work, their bosses wanted them sober; hungover workers caused too many accidents.

The banish-the-bar strategy was too short-sighted for some churchmen, who felt liquor-selling grocery stores were a more insidious threat. Not only were stores more convenient and comfortable than downtown bars, but also the store-purchased booze was cheaper than saloon booze. At a bar, gulping back 26 ounces at 25 cents a slug cost about $3.25. A store-bought 26-ounce bottle cost less than $1.50.

Temperance Brigades

About the time Cameron took his Saturday-night survey, teetotalling Protestant clergymen sought to address drinking through their Manitoba Temperance Alliance. Meanwhile, Presbyterian ministers joined with Catholic,

Anglican and Methodist church leaders to form the Manitoba branch of the Dominion Temperance Alliance (DTA). Temperance meant just that: a movement to encourage *reasonable, restrained* use of liquor on an individual basis, rather than through outright government bans. Churchmen urged the enforcement of Winnipeg hotel and liquor bylaws and pressed the provincial government to enforce liquor traffic regulations already on the books. The DTA went further, demanding the provincial government limit the number of hotels and advocating an end to grocery-store liquor sales. Alas, in an era when only men could cast ballots, vote-hungry politicians were not eager to enforce existing laws, let alone write new ones, lest they alienate hard-drinking voters.

Even when conditions became so intolerable that civic leaders were forced to take action, the outcomes were sometimes disheartening. In Portage la Prairie, police arrested barkeeps under a town bylaw. All were convicted and fined. The barkeeps appealed their convictions and won on the grounds that the city had exceeded its authority. Adding insult to injury, the appeal judge ordered the magistrate who had presided at the original trial to pay court costs. In an emergency convention, the Manitoba DTA branch voted to raise the required $1,500, so the magistrate wouldn't have to sell his home to pay the legal tab.

In 1907, in Alberta, W.G.W. Fortune founded what he called the Temperance and Moral Reform League. Like churchmen in Manitoba, Fortune and others urged church-going drinkers to sign total abstinence pledges and to join the Anti-treating League. Members were invited to carry cards with which to fend off "friends" who coerced them into bars and saloons. The powerful lobby group United Farmers of Alberta (UFA) gave its support. However, not even the UFA could change the nature of male social pressure, and the league failed. Although many of its demands were adopted years later, Manitoba's DTA branch did not survive, not because its war on whisky was unpopular, but because its cause was sidelined by divisive school and language warfare between Protestants and Catholics.

Added to the temperance advocates' frustration with the human frailty of drinkers and, occasionally, the beaten wives who came to the defence of drunken husbands, was another frustration the NWMP knew only too well. Governments were indifferent in the face of more pressing issues of the day, showing a sometimes shocking lack of insight, or worse, rank incompetence. New legislation sometimes exacerbated the problem it was meant to solve. Back in 1887, at the recommendation of temperance leaders, North-West Territories' Lieutenant-Governor Joseph Royal legalized 4 percent beer as a substitute for whisky. He also inexplicably made whisky importation permits easier to obtain. The result was that territorial whisky importation skyrocketed from just over 21,000 gallons in 1887 to over 151,000 gallons just two years later.

Politicians backed away from mounting prohibition pressure. By 1898, Prime Minister Wilfrid Laurier had ignored pleas for a national law for two years. Did the majority of Canadians really want prohibition? Laurier finally suggested a plebiscite to answer the question. When the results of the all-male vote were tabulated, temperance advocates rejoiced: 278,380 votes were cast in favour of national prohibition and 264,693 against. All provinces except Catholic-influenced Quebec voted dry, with residents in the prairie provinces voting three to one to outlaw booze. Quebec's wet result (122,760 votes) narrowed the prohibitionists' majority to a slim 13,687 votes, but it *was* a clear majority.

Laurier's response left temperance advocates stunned. In the prime minister's eyes, the plebiscite was, in effect, a defeat for prohibition! Why, 13,687 votes represented a mere 23 percent of the total Canadian electorate—and a whole lot less of the electorate in Quebec. Laurier refused to discuss the issue further. Soon, the forces of prohibition knew they would obtain little help from the federal government. Increasingly, they focused their energies on persuading their respective provincial governments.

Sisters of Sobriety
Since the 1880s, Canadian women had looked to the US temperance movement for both inspiration and ammunition. Slim, bespectacled Frances Willard, the national

president of the Women's Christian Temperance Union
(WCTU), crossed the border to help establish the women's
organization on the prairies. American temperance pro-
paganda was widely distributed in Willard's wake. Prairie
newspapers, which rarely refused free handouts, printed
much of it. These features made for entertaining read-
ing, illustrated as they were with horror stories of families
burned or frozen to death, or children dying of starvation
or cold as fathers drank themselves into a stupor.

Despite small population centres, the WCTU was flour-
ishing on the prairies by 1917. That year, Saskatchewan alone
claimed over 1,600 members registered in 73 local unions
throughout six districts. The Band of Hope, the Loyal
Temperance Legion and other temperance school groups
were organized. Kids listened as earnest women spoke, then
sang songs and munched cookies. Many of these same children accompanied parents to temperance and prohibition
rallies, where they fervently applauded stirring speakers
and joined in on songs such as "Lips That Touch Liquor
Shall Never Touch Mine" and "Father, Dear Father:"

> Our fire has gone out—our house is all dark—
> And mother's been watching since tea.
> With poor brother Benny so sick in her arms
> And no one to help her but me.
> Come home! Come home! Come home,
> Please, father, dear father, come home.

Hillhurst Presbyterian Sunday School administrators and students "get out the dry vote" in Calgary in 1915. GLENBOW ARCHIVES NA-1639-2

By the end of this excruciating song-saga (and while father was still presumably knocking back the booze), sickly brother Benny had been transported away by "the angels of light," a tragic fate that reduced many overwrought singers to tears. James Gray admitted that the song struck so close to home that he was in his late teens before he could hear it without "bawling unashamedly."

In the years following 1890, when the WCTU inaugurated a national prohibition campaign, a handful of determined, outspoken women, including Nellie McClung in Manitoba, Louise McKinney and Emily Murphy in Alberta and Violet McNaughton in Saskatchewan supported the cause. However, some of these women had another far more important agenda: women's suffrage—the right to vote. At the time, women were unable to cast a ballot provincially or federally. For many, suffrage, not temperance, had been their first call to activism. Nellie McClung's initial public-speaking engagement was during a 1907 WCTU temperance convention, but suffragette McClung talked about whisky, not votes. "It is easy to see why we concentrated on the liquor traffic," she explained years later. "It was corporeal and always present; it walked our streets; it threw its challenge in our faces!"

McClung soon discovered stumping for prohibition could be profitable. While she fervently believed in the cause, the bestselling novelist knew that her written words were worth something more than mere plaudits and applause, so why not her spoken words? Prohibitionists obviously concurred and shelled out up to $200 a week—more than many people earned in a month—for Nellie's time behind the podium at rural rallies.

The motivation for both temperance advocates and suffrage supporters was not reforming drinkers, but their mutual interest in improving the status and lives of women. In that spirit, prairie WCTU organizations later supported women's suffrage, with temperance advocate Violet McNaughton initiating a broadly based 1909 campaign that inundated Saskatchewan's provincial government with over 100 lengthy suffrage petitions from dozens of rural constituencies.

Suffragettes had no hidden agenda; obtaining the

vote for women was their publicly avowed objective. McNaughton and other temperance leaders realized that simply launching "frontal assaults" on drink would not necessarily win their own war, but obtaining suffrage just might win the battle of the bottle, not only by making it possible for women to elect male temperance sympathizers to office, but also by electing women to champion the temperance cause as MLAs and MPs. Such sentiments flew in the face of reality: male voters had already won—and lost—Laurier's 1898 clear majority plebiscite. The issue of prohibition obviously transcended gender. That was actually fortunate for prohibitionists. As the 20th century dawned over the Canadian west, men still outnumbered women.

In any case, in Alberta, suffrage advocates never got the opportunity to put their theories to the test. Both McClung and McKinney became Alberta MLAs, but won their seats in the Alberta Legislature after prohibition had already been officially endorsed by men. The Manitoba and Saskatchewan plebiscites that later inscribed prohibition into law were held just after women received their provincial franchises. Did those results hinge on female voters? Not likely, for if most men had voted wet, prohibition would likely have gone down to defeat. But men—including the vast majority of drinkers—voted dry in huge numbers. To what extent women, and in particular the WCTU, influenced their decision to do so has been a matter of debate ever since.

5

A New Dawn
in the West

JANUARY 1, 1904, WAS FAST approaching. Bob Edwards, the big, bluff editor and proprietor of Calgary's insightful, hilarious *Eye Opener* newspaper, had a heartfelt suggestion for his readers' New Year's resolution. The idea probably came to Edwards without too much reflection. The subject was ever-present in his mind and never more so than during the annual holiday season. He and thousands of other western Canadian men had just staggered through the year's biggest single excuse for drinking. Edwards sat down heavily behind his desk and picked up his pen.

"Swear off," he wrote in a shaky hand. "Climb into the water wagon. Life is a one-sided fight for the man who is his worst enemy. Swear off. If you make one hundred good resolutions and only keep one, you are just that much better off. But let that one be booze. The others will follow. We speak with authority."

During the 20-year run of the disarmingly frank *Eye Opener*, Bob Edwards spoke "with authority" on a seemingly endless number of topics, including gossip ("Any man who repeats half of what he hears talks too much"), faith ("Faith is the belief in something you know isn't so"), doctors ("Heart failure covers a lot of medical ignorance"), gambling ("Success at poker depends on the way a man is raised"), politics ("Politics, you will observe, is the science of guessing right") and women ("Never judge a woman by the company she is compelled to entertain").

The above aphorisms hint that the *Eye Opener* was not, in the usual sense, a newspaper at all, but in this pre-electronic age, a primitive printing-press blog. The journal's two-decade lifespan is misleading. Between its first issue in 1902 and its last in 1922, the newspaper occasionally made no appearance at all for weeks at a time. Many loyal readers knew the reason, and most others guessed: Bob had fallen off the wagon again and was recovering in a hospital somewhere. Bob usually provided an explanation for the paper's absence himself in its next, long-awaited issue. Few other topics appeared so frequently in the *Eye Opener*'s pages as booze and drunkenness, including Bob's own:

We held the bottle up and took
A brief and scrutinizing look,
And then we put the thing away
And muttered hoarsely, "Not today."

The *Eye Opener* was just a few months old when Edwards used readers' criticisms to shed a perceptive light on the prevailing small-town social scene:

> We are sometimes upbraided for featuring booze and the bar in these columns. What would you have us write about? We have to write about what goes on around us and it cannot be disputed that the bar is the centre of social life in small western burgs. There is no town society in the usual acceptation of the term. It is a very extraordinary occasion when a High River young man finds himself sitting in the parlor of a private home talking to the ladies. He is never asked.
>
> The bar is bright and cheery and always on the spot and also touches the spot. The man craving human companionship can always find some of the gang there and the throb of the human heart. He finds, too, in the bartender, one who understands his wants and laughs at his jokes. Oh, yes, the bar's all right.

Bob Edwards's Big Decision

As early as 1908, with prohibition forces girding for whisky warfare, Bob Edwards appeared to approve of their single-minded determination to rid society of alcohol. "The *Eye Opener* has no defence to offer for the booze traffic," he told his more than 18,000 readers. "It is a bad business; none worse. We've been there. Nobody can tell us a thing about it we don't already know and our frank opinion is that the complete abolition of strong drink would solve the problem of the world's happiness."

Like many others, Bob Edwards grew impatient with the pious attitudes of some prohibitionists, and he let them know it some years after prohibition was law. "There is no use trying to be funny about prohibition. To the wets there is nothing funny about the dry situation and the prohibitionists never see any humour in anything."

As the war between Alberta's wets and drys intensified in the months leading up to the long-anticipated 1915 provincial prohibition plebiscite, Bob followed the skirmishes intensely—and so did his tens of thousands of readers. On the *Eye Opener*'s tenth anniversary, in 1912, Edwards claimed a circulation of 35,000, "all over the dominion," rivalling that of the *Toronto Daily Star*. Only the three dailies in western Canada's largest city, Winnipeg, enjoyed a larger western Canadian reach. The *Eye Opener*'s influence was felt beyond Canada's borders. In Britain, it helped define Calgary itself ("the place where the *Eye Opener* comes from"), and a New York literary journal applauded the editor/publisher's "clear judgement and common sense." But the whisky wars sorely tested both these Edwards attributes. Readers everywhere wondered which side alcoholic Bob Edwards would endorse. Both wets and drys attempted to curry Bob's favour.

A deputation of worried hotelmen and liquor wholesalers visited the editor to confirm his support for wets. Bob worried them even more by saying he was inclined to support the new Alberta Liquor Act, which would impose a stringent 2.5-percent alcohol limit in any beverage.

"Bob, you could use some money," one of them reportedly told the editor. "Wouldn't five or ten thousand dollars help you a lot?" Could Edwards use some *money*? Would it *help*? For the man who later lamented that, "If money talks, all it ever said to me was 'good-bye,'" the wets' proposition held a good deal of appeal.

As a wet-supporting journal, the *Eye Opener* would be in good company. While the second-rank papers *Edmonton Bulletin* and *Calgary Albertan* were dry, the two major Alberta dailies, *Edmonton Journal* and *Calgary Herald*, were solidly on the side of the wets. But where did the *Eye Opener* stand? Nobody was sure. In his columns, Edwards had from time to time pointed a ridiculing finger at both sides. Ah, but the money!

"Yes, I could use it," Bob admitted, "but I've never taken that kind of money and I would not accept it now. Gentlemen, my mind is made up." But what did "made up" mean? Bob let the liquor men wonder and worry some more.

A short time later, representatives from the Temperance and Moral Reform League walked into Edwards's office. Prohibitionists had worked long and hard on their campaign. The United Grain Growers of Alberta endorsed their plan, as did the Alberta Medical Association. The summer before, over 500 canvassers had pounded the pavement in search of support for legislation. In order to pressure the provincial government to hold a plebiscite on the issue, they had gathered thousands more names than the government regulations required. Edwards admired that kind of affirmative action, but he wasn't about to let the drys off easily.

Edwards spoke first. "You're after my support?" he asked the prohibitionists. "The wets would pay me well. How much is it worth to you?"

There were frowns and nervous glances. "We're sorry, Mr. Edwards, but we have no money."

Bob nodded. "That's fine," he said, "because I'm not for sale. I'm with you. The next issue of the *Eye Opener* will make that very clear."

As usual, Bob wrote his next Saturday edition on Tuesday night. What he produced in those late-evening hours was, according to popular Alberta historian Grant MacEwan, "perhaps the most influential editorial penned in the New West up to that time." Once it was done, Edwards delivered his prose to the offices of the *Albertan* for typesetting. Shortly after that, as MacEwan delicately phrased it, "Bob Edwards yielded to his old enemy and lost all interest in publication." The reason, MacEwan suggests, was that companionable wets offered the editor a drink, and Bob accepted, perhaps to reward himself for a job well done. One drink, as usual, led to another.

What the wets hadn't counted on was the loyalty Bob Edwards inspired in his colleagues. On Thursday, the print manager approached Arthur Halpen, assistant foreman in the composing room. "Bob has seen his galley proofs but now he's half drunk; could you handle the make-up of his pages?" Halpen knew Bob's layout well, agreed he could do it and then took the results to Bob himself, whom he found slouched in his office chair.

Banishing Arthur to the player piano that sat in the corner, Bob reached for his marking pencil and, while the ivories beat out their mechanical cadences, slashed red strokes across the pages, killing the edition. In his stupor, the editor had decided there would be no *Eye Opener* that crucial week before the plebiscite vote. Then he calmly poured himself another drink.

But *Albertan* editor W.M. Davidson decided he had a mandate to see his friend's newspaper printed. Davidson, Halpen and the *Eye Opener*'s indefatigable secretary, Bertha Hart, read and corrected the proofs, and then the presses rolled. The next day, desperate hotelmen visited Bertha, offering to write a cheque for the entire edition, simply to keep it from the public. She refused their offer. Taking no chances, Davidson spirited out-of-town copies safely away and locked all Calgary copies in his vault. On early Saturday morning, July 17, 1915, newsboys snatched up their copies from the *Eye Opener*'s office and hit the streets.

Prohibition's Losers and Winners

While Bob Edwards lay in a Calgary hospital bed, *Eye Opener* readers in the city, throughout Alberta and in many distant parts of Canada, read his words. "Consider well," Bob began, spelling out the consequences of prohibition:

> Many hotelmen will be put out of business and placed in grave financial difficulties. They are to get no compensation. Engaged in an occupation that is legalized and specifically licensed by the government and the city, they suddenly find the earth opening up at their feet and a yawning pit of utter ruin being prepared for them to fall into, held the while at the mercy of rapacious landlords, inexorable temperance workers and absolutely heartless bankers. Does this not excite your pity?
>
> It does ours, but only to a limited extent, for a panorama passes before our eyes of women and little children in humble homes, shy proper food and clothing, lacking warmth in winter and bereft completely of the joy of living, going to sleep in misery and awakening to another day with the dull pain of hopelessness, innocent victims of the damnable traffic of booze; see a multitude of downcast men, down-and-outers, panhandling for dimes on the street to procure more of that very booze which lost them every job they ever had.

Bob's "panorama" also included "poor devils of both sexes being yanked each night to the police station and chucked into cells; to meet further humiliation the next morning in the dock," and finally, "the pitiful vision of graves containing the remains of men, good men . . . brought to an abrupt and shameful conclusion by bad whiskey and by nothing else. In a word," he concluded, "There is death in the Cup, and if this [prohibition] Act is likely to have the effect of dashing the Cup from the drunkard's hand, for God's sake let us vote for it."

Voting In a New Way of Life

On Wednesday, July 21, four days after the *Eye Opener*'s prohibition edition was distributed, Alberta men went to the polls as never before. There were 140,000 registered voters in the province. A stunning 70 percent of them marked ballots. The prohibitionists won the day, 58,295 to 37,508. They swept the rural areas, as they expected, but the real surprise was that four of the province's five major cities also voted dry. Only Lethbridge voted wet, like the tiny Crowsnest Pass coal towns to the west and some isolated communities in the north. The bars would be closed up tight on July 1 (or, as the *Lethbridge Herald* dubbed it, "July the Thirst").

Almost 20 years before in Manitoba, the leader of the opposition, "Wet" Rodmond Roblin, had been prohibitionists' worst enemy. To win the 1899 provincial election, his own party persuaded Roblin to step aside so it could replace him with a dry proponent, Hugh Macdonald, the son of Sir John A. Macdonald. It was a good strategy: Macdonald's Conservatives swept into power. Macdonald produced what was known variously as the "Macdonald Act" and the "Prohibitionists' Magna Carta." It was passed into law in 1900. Prohibition had arrived—at least on paper.

While Macdonald was persuaded to go on to bigger and better things as a candidate in the upcoming federal election, Roblin, the man who once deemed destructive barroom treating as "the manifestation of the social and intellectual qualities of man," slipped back in as Manitoba premier. Roblin stalled on ratifying prohibition by suggesting the province needed an up-to-date plebiscite on the issue. Time passed, but there was no move to enact Macdonald's prohibition law.

By 1914, the prohibition issue was all but overshadowed by a Conservative corruption scandal regarding the letting of contracts for the construction of the new Manitoba legislative buildings. Roblin was forced to resign. Liberal leader Tobias Norris took up the sword of temperance, promising a referendum on the issue. Just days before Alberta's prohibition plebiscite, Norris's Liberals won the provincial election in a landslide. The new government chose March 13, 1916, as plebiscite day.

That winter, the WCTU stuffed mailboxes, erected billboards and held rallies. All but two of Manitoba's newspapers joined the dry crusade (the two wets were Catholic newspapers, concerned, it seemed, about access to wine for the sacrament). Virtually any organization with any broad-based clout—the Grain Growers, the

Retail Merchants Association and even the Conservative opposition party—helped hoist prohibition's banner. In spite of some exceptions, including, to no one's surprise, the Bartenders' Union, labour organizations rallied to the cause. Churchmen preached the dry gospel from their pulpits, and guest speakers, including Nellie McClung, added oratory fuel to the fire. When ballots were counted, 43 of the province's 46 constituencies had voted dry. Manitoba's new premier, Toby Norris, blew the dust off Macdonald's old "Magna Carta," and made ready to close the bars.

Bracketed by provinces that had outlawed alcoholic beverages, Saskatchewan residents readied themselves for their own prohibition plebiscite on December 11, 1916. Saskatchewan premier Walter Scott had already made one monumental decision that shortened his province's journey to prohibition. Like Manitoba's Roblin, Scott was no friend of temperance or prohibition. Earlier, he had arbitrarily set the minimum number of dry votes in a potential plebiscite at 50,000 before his government would take action. The number was too high, complained prohibitionists. Scott shrugged and simply withdrew the plebiscite offer. It was strange, then, that in 1915, Scott announced that on Dominion Day, the government would close every bar in the province. What a holiday for the drys!

In the place of bars, government-controlled dispensaries were to be established. The government would also test the whisky sold to make sure customers could buy it without fear of going blind. On July 1, 1915, 406 bars, 38 liquor wholesalers and 12 clubs were shuttered. In Saskatoon, a Methodist minister discovered there was good reason for hallelujahs: 20 bars and 4 wholesalers had been replaced by just one new government outlet.

The motive for Scott's flip-flop was never convincingly explained, but who really understood the workings of this manic depressive's brain? Only the naive would suggest that the premier acted with the best interests of Saskatchewan families at heart. Scott—or those close to him—likely felt the winds of change and knew which way they were blowing. Perhaps Walter Scott had better-honed political survival instincts than other political leaders. Ironically, the premier's about-face made him, in effect, a prohibition leader. Regardless of how hard Alberta's prohibitionists campaigned, it was Saskatchewan's bar closings that helped prompt Alberta's government to hold its own plebiscite.

Now, a year later, Saskatchewan citizens lined up to vote for a new way of life. Having won their suffrage just nine months before, thousands of women joined the queues. They resoundingly voted for *total* prohibition by a landslide 95,249 to 23,666 votes, even tossing out the government's own liquor dispensaries. From Banff, Alberta, to Winnipeg, Manitoba, the Canadian prairies were formally dry.

6

Life in the Dry World

CALGARY POLICE CHIEF ALFRED CUDDY wrote his 1917 annual report with decidedly mixed emotions. The statistics told the tale: arrests for drunkenness had plummeted from 1,743 in 1914, the year before the prohibition plebiscite, to a mere 183 by the end of 1917. The prohibitionists were mighty happy, but if there was a smile on Chief Cuddy's face, it was an uneasy one. While his report concluded that prohibition had produced a drop not only in drunkenness, but also in every type of crime in the city, any pleasure Cuddy took from recording the fact was balanced by other realities. Reduced crime rates were the effect of the change in law, not a result of more effective law enforcement. Another reality was that in the wake of a real estate crash, many prairie towns and cities were owed millions in uncollectable taxes. Calgary was no exception. Belt-tightening measures were the order of the day, and prohibition-era police departments were the politician's favourite target.

When funding was cut, so were positions on the force. Sixty-three constables had once pounded Calgary's pavements. By late 1917, there were just 28 names on the duty rosters. In less than two years, 35 men had suddenly found themselves out of a job, the poor sods. One of the city's four district police stations had been closed, providing tangible proof of Cuddy's shrinking police department.

Law-enforcement officers everywhere witnessed prohibition's early effects. Inspector West of the Royal North West Mounted Police (RNWMP) in Battleford, Saskatchewan division, noted that loafers and drunks had disappeared from town streets, and the pleasantly surprised municipal authorities reported that 1916 tax payments had shot up by 95 percent. Inspector Spalding in Moose Jaw considered prohibition the reason that crime in his area was down a stunning 75 percent. Little wonder Saskatchewan closed one of its near-empty provincial jails. Poverty was down, too. Spalding reported only three or four cases of destitution, instead of the dozens dealt with in previous years.

Prohibition's effect in Manitoba was unbelievable. In 1913, courtrooms and jails throughout the province were crowded with 7,493 drunks. In prohibition's first year, only 1,085 hungover men stood contritely before judges. Far fewer men were arrested for violent crime, as well. Manitoba did Saskatchewan one better and closed two provincial jails.

The Thirsty West

Bars and saloons were crowded and noisy one night and locked up tight and silent the next. With that, the drinking man's way of life ended—cold turkey. Employees left work with their paycheques in their pockets and walked straight home. One happy consequence of this was experienced by Alberta's bankers. Inside their sandstone-faced establishments, long lines of depositors stood waiting to get to the wickets. Just one month after prohibition started, savings at the province's banks had almost doubled.

What Canadian history does not record is the effect prohibition had inside countless Canadian prairie homes. In 1982's *Bacchanalia Revisited*, James Gray gives us a hint of prohibition's stunning impact on his own family: "Like so many thousands of other drunks, my father was a fervent prohibitionist because he believed if the bars were shut he and others like him would be rescued," Gray remembered. "My father was dead right about the bars. When the bars were closed in 1916, he got a steady job, kept it, and brought his pay home every week. The early prohibition years from 1916 to 1920 were the best years of our lives."

There were many more drinkers out there than anyone could see. In one of the most lasting effects of prohibition, drinkers simply moved from the bars and streets into their own homes, a change that spawned another phenomenon: the woman drinker.

Women—even prostitutes—rarely frequented bars, which were traditionally male enclaves. However, in the privacy of her home, a woman could discreetly fill her glass again and again. The alcohol women had previously consumed was in the guise of medicinal remedies available at every drugstore. The most potent were Hall's Great Discovery (43 percent alcohol), Hostetter's Bitters (46 percent) and Hamlin's Wizard Oil (containing an astonishing 65 percent). Emboldened by their successful bid to vote, more and more women began to substitute undisguised booze for former remedies. Judging by the amount of alcohol many had been ingesting in the name of good health, having a drink or two in the evenings was, by comparison, almost tantamount to taking "the pledge."

Like their male counterparts, women discovered that solitary drinking was much less fun than drinking with friends. As usual, Bob Edwards of the *Eye Opener* dutifully mocked the trend: "Society Note—The bridge party which was to have been given by Mrs. Peter McSnuffy at her charming residence on Mount Royal last Wednesday had to be called off at the last minute. The whiskey laid in for the occasion had inadvertently been lapped up by McSnuffy the previous evening."

In order to drink, of course, law-abiding citizens had to buy booze. If it was outlawed, how and where were they getting it? Early on, some feared an invasion of American rum-runners. (The name is a misnomer; the preferred merchandise was always whisky.) However, any entrepreneurial American would have frowned at the profit-making prospects. Lethbridge, the "big city" a short drive from Montana, had a population of just 32,000 in 1916. Regina, roughly the same distance from the border, was even smaller, with 26,000 people. Moose Jaw was a town of just 17,000 citizens. In addition, First World War–era census figures are misleading; names were there, but thousands of men had left for Europe to fight the Hun. Moose Jaw's absent soldiers (most of them drinkers) accounted for an astonishing one-sixth of its population. Even if they chose to operate in a foreign country patrolled by the redoubtable Mounties, savvy Americans quickly realized that the Canadian prairies were not only short on people, they were long on distances, especially those they would have to travel to hit Calgary and Edmonton. The American rum-runner invasion never materialized.

Among the most successful Canadian rum-runners were railway men, who used the trains, stashing liquor inside hog and cattle carcasses, buried in tons of coal and even in a carload of dynamite. Bootlegging—the manufacture or selling of illicit liquor—existed in the countryside and in some cities (18 stills were raided in an early 1919 Edmonton operation), but secret stills were usually small, homemade affairs, incapable of mass production. An exception was the 500-gallon-a-day distillery dug into a hillside southeast of Medicine Hat. Stills were uncovered in the unlikeliest places: an empty Methodist Church in Ranchville, Saskatchewan, and a stable in Drumheller, Alberta. The Calgary bootleg operation in an empty store on 17th Avenue West that Chief Cuddy and his men knocked over in 1918 was bigger than most, producing 75 gallons of full-strength beer a week, but that represented mere drops compared with the oceans consumed each week before pro-hibition. Without the time or resources to transport their product anywhere, most bootleggers simply waited for their few dozen customers to come to them.

Western Canadians didn't have to hope for American rum-runners to supply them. They didn't have to take chances with the dubious quality of most bootleggers' expensive homemade hooch, either. Within a few weeks of the bar closures, imbibers were pleasantly surprised to dis-cover that governments were still on the drinker's side.

Beer-drinkers had it the easiest. Most cities had brewer-ies, and because they were federally licensed, provinces were powerless to shut them down. As prohibition descended, many simply switched to producing the temperance beer, with less than 1.2 percent alcohol content, that provincial governments still allowed. Nobody was happier about that than the good citizens of Lethbridge. It wasn't just that they had a ready source of pseudo-suds, it was also because the brewery happened to be one of the city's biggest industries.

This attic still was uncovered by Edmonton police in early 1919. James H. Gray estimated its output at 200 gallons of whisky a week.
GLENBOW ARCHIVES NC-6-4040

German-born Fritz Sick had established the Lethbridge Brewing and Malting Co. Ltd. early in the century. By 1912, it was producing 100,000 barrels of beer annually in an operation that sprawled across several city blocks. A new brand was born: Old Style Pilsner, with each bottle bearing the evocative label that to this day reflects the bygone western era of its founding. What helped Sick considerably was that Lethbridge Brewing had developed a sizeable export trade in full-strength beer. Sick successfully rode out the first years of Canadian prohibition by exporting the real stuff across the line, while selling temperance beer at home. Prohibition offered opportunity; Sick bought one of the three breweries that Saskatchewan's Prohibition Act had shuttered. In 1923, he built another in Prince Albert. Two years later, he and his son took over the Edmonton Brewing and Malting Company.

If you were a hard-liquor man, prohibition didn't stop you from slaking your thirst, either. Affluent drinkers had the means—and ample opportunity before the law changed—to stock up. Shelving was hammered together as tool sheds and root cellars became walk-in liquor pantries. Wholesalers filled personal orders by the caseload. The phenomenon didn't go unnoticed by Bob Edwards, whose *Eye Opener* lampooned the mania: "The many friends of Martin M. Bingham will be sorry to learn that he fell down a steep flight of steps Wednesday and broke his neck. Mr. Bingham was in the act of lowering a case of Three Star Hennessey into the cellar when his foot slipped. It is understood that the Hennessey was three years old and will revert to his widow. The bereaved woman is receiving many callers."

The new law allowed liquor purchases for "medicinal purposes." Government outlets were established in both Edmonton and Calgary to provide such liquor. In Edmonton, the appointed vendor earning a government stipend was Reverend W. F. Gold, former secretary of the Temperance and Moral Reform League. In Calgary, it was that old Morley missionary, Reverend McDougall. In the minds of some, profiting from prohibition put these pious gentlemen in the same league as bootleggers. In the minds of Gold and McDougall, it likely was more about enabling controlled consumption than personal gain from the $1,800 annual stipend. What happened next made that contention laughable.

For working stiffs who didn't have a hope of turning their cellars into liquor warehouses, bottles were as close as their nearest drugstore. All that was needed was a prescription from the friendly family doctor, who was likely seeing more "patients" than ever before. Typical visits were short; a couple of minutes later, the healthy individual was striding to the drugstore for a bottle of "good for what ails ya." In tiny Peace River Crossing, a town of a few hundred souls, residents handed liquor-dispensing pharmacists 1,008 prescriptions in a single month. The government fought back by issuing numbered prescription pads, but soon thousands of clever forgeries were sliding across drugstore counters.

More serious was the federal law that allowed liquor to be legally imported across provincial borders. Drinkers who no longer could buy a drink at a bar or a bottle at a grocery store, could simply telephone a wholesaler in the next province and have their order shipped in, albeit one bottle at a time. In Saskatoon, you might live just a few minutes' drive from liquor wholesaler Nat Bell, who couldn't sell you anything but was shipping direct from his warehouse to folks in Lethbridge. Never mind; Calgary's Diamond Brothers would happily fill your order and ship it to Saskatoon. Many express depots or post offices began resembling liquor stores. Getting a drink wasn't as simple as walking into a bar, but most people judged the inconvenience a minor one and merely counted their blessings as they lifted a glass.

The Dry Squad

Just a few months into prohibition, it became apparent to prohibitionists that laws were useless unless they were vigorously enforced, and enforcement wasn't happening. Aside from the occasional headline-grabbing bootlegger raid—with crime so low, newspapers were desperate for any front-page material—police did little and greeted criticism with a shrug. Few police departments now had the manpower to pursue bootleggers and rum-runners in the way prohibitionists expected. Besides, many men who pounded the beat all day also pounded back the booze all night, so prohibition duties were decidedly hypocritical.

Social Service Council members pleaded with Winnipeg city council to beef up enforcement. Go see the provincial government, which collects bootleggers' fines, the finance committee chairman advised. In Alberta, prohibitionists did just that. Five hundred WCTU and Social Service League members rallied at the legislature, demanding loopholes be closed and the law enforced. Premier Arthur Sifton stalled. The man who finally forced Sifton's hand was, ironically, the commissioner of the RNWMP. Aylesworth Bowen Perry took matters into his own hands, and in doing so, saved the reputation of the legendary "Scarlet Force."

If city police and provincial governments couldn't or wouldn't enforce prohibition effectively, Perry knew it wouldn't be long before people turned to the RNWMP to do the job. Perry's concern about liquor enforcement was decades old. As superintendent at Prince Albert, Saskatchewan, in the late 1880s, he had admitted to his superiors that his detachment had a difficult time simply proving breweries were selling full-strength beer. While ardent prohibitionists might applaud the force's liquor enforcement efforts, Perry knew the general public would not. There had been no applause for the Mounties' efforts in the 1880s, and he knew he wouldn't hear any this time around. Perry feared the RNWMP would be drawn into the liquor war again, a war he knew it could not win. Fortunately for the commissioner and his men, a much more important war was currently being waged.

By the First World War, Canada's population included a significant number of German immigrants and even more citizens of German heritage. Who knew what they might be plotting? Anti-German hysteria was enough to fire up Calgary mobs who trashed a German-owned restaurant and hotel. At a time when one-third of the force's former rank-and-file was now wearing khaki instead of red serge, members of the undermanned force were being seconded to reinforce border patrols and to undertake what are now called "covert activities" in attempts to ferret out potential German threats.

In 1916, when the federal government asked Perry's

opinion on undertaking additional espionage and surveillance duties, he suggested that the Mounties could only accomplish this if relieved of their provincial policing duties—which included enforcing provincial prohibition. In the meantime, Perry wanted to discourage provinces from expecting liquor patrols from his eager-to-please policemen. "No instruction whatever has been issued by me in regard to this," he reminded his senior officers in Alberta. Unless otherwise notified, Perry told them unequivocally, prohibition "is not be enforced by the Mounted Police."

National security was clearly the federal government's priority; it wanted its national police fighting threats from foreigners, not knocking over stills and collaring suspected rum-runners. Perry's ally in this was none other than his political boss, Director-General of the National Service (later prime minister) R.B. Bennett. In Bennett's mind, the stalwart Mounties were above undignified duties that had them "go out and search for a quart of beer or a pint of Whiskey." When Alberta and Saskatchewan RNWMP contracts came to an end in 1917, they were not renewed.

Setting a precedent for Saskatchewan and Alberta, British Columbia had formed its own provincial police force in 1858, and the Manitoba Provincial Police had been operating since 1871. Saskatchewan premier Walter Scott had wanted his own police force since 1914. On January 1, 1917, he got it. It was a bad bargain: the RNWMP had cost Saskatchewan just $200,000 a year for the services of hundreds of personnel.

The new Saskatchewan Provincial Police (SPP) cost the province $500,000 for a thinly spread force of just 175 officers and men. Financial realities for the new Alberta Provincial Police (APP) were even worse. The Mounties had cost Alberta just $75,000 a year. Now the tab was $300,000.

Organizing the new forces was a mad scramble. Time was not the only enemy. Many applicants were rejected out of hand. Most able-bodied prairie men were now in Flanders, stoically advancing across no-man's land in the face of withering machine-gun fire. The infant provincial forces had more than a manpower problem; chronically short of funds, they couldn't have hired more men even if better applicants had been available. The result was one-man detachments responsible for territories as large as 1,000 square miles, investigating all manner of crime, from cattle rustling to murder. One lone APP officer patrolled the Montana border between British Columbia and Saskatchewan. Bootleggers and rum-runners laughed.

However, the situation was no laughing matter for most prairie residents. Suddenly, priorities shifted from prohibition enforcement to basic peacekeeping. By 1918, Alberta MLAs from Edmonton, Okotoks and Pincher Creek reported their constituents wanted the Mounties back. Crime had quadrupled since they had left. In 1917, the United Farmers of Alberta had passed a convention resolution that amounted to a Mountie ultimatum: enforce prohibition or get out. A year later, worried rural residents were reconsidering. At the next convention, one farmer spoke for many when he shouted, "One redcoat is better than the whole provincial police force!" In the following months, things went from bad to worse for the APP. Internal feuding between the superintendent and his assistant sparked the resignation of 53 men.

In 1918, Alberta's Attorney General, John R. Boyle, fought a furious "letter war" in the *Lethbridge Herald* with the mayor of the wet-voting city, W.D.L. Hardie. Lethbridge had become a "rendezvous for gamblers, crooks and criminals," Boyle thundered. Hardie replied that the city "didn't have money to burn" for extra policemen to augment the two constables and detective now led by the fire chief (who was doing double duty since the previous chief had gone to war with the Lethbridge Highlanders). The Social Service League put on the pressure, and Boyle was forced to send in a special plainclothes squad. Twelve of the 60 men taken into custody at two gambling houses turned out to be bootleggers. Arrests were one thing, but how were meaningful convictions possible, former WCTU president and newly elected MLA Louise McKinney wondered, when the judges presiding over liquor cases had been drunk the night before?

There is no record of Commissioner Bowen Perry's reaction to all this. The complaints and concerns might well have been a source of grim satisfaction. They were proof that the RNWMP was seen not only to "Maintain the Right," as its motto stated, but that his beleaguered force also had managed to maintain its integrity and reputation.

7

King of the Boozoriums

IN 1889, RUSSIAN LANDHOLDER Yechiel Bronfman made the biggest decision of his life. Sacrificing his grist mill and tobacco plantation, Bronfman, pregnant wife Minnie, daughter Laura and sons Abe and Harry fled the destruction and rape of vicious anti-Semitic pogroms. The family settled in what would one day be eastern Saskatchewan. By the time they stepped off the train, the three Bronfman kids had a newborn baby brother, Sam.

Ever since those hard-scrabble times, Yechiel—or Ekiel, as he was called in Canada—had made one money-making decision after another. He'd left an unproductive farm to make money in town, become a peddler, bought cheap wood and become a fuel merchant, and started a delivery service.

He also bought wild horses brought up by American cowboys from Montana and South Dakota and, after second son Harry broke them in, sold them as docile harness animals.

As was the custom at the conclusion of a horse-buying session, Bronfman and the cowboys would leave bronco-bustin' Harry at the corral and amble into the bar of the Langham Hotel to buy a round of drinks. One day, young Sam followed them and peeked inside. Sam perceived something in that smoky, noisy room that his father had not yet understood. Ekiel saw the same thing Sam did: thirsty men lined up and waiting to get to the bar, but it was Sam who recognized an opportunity to make real money. "The Langham bar makes more profit than we do, Father," Sam recalled telling Ekiel. "Instead of selling horses, we should be selling drinks."

Ekiel soon mortgaged the family home, persuaded a brewer to stake him and became the proud owner of the Anglo-American Hotel in Emerson, Manitoba. It's easy to conclude that it was simple money-making acumen that propelled Ekiel's boys down the profitable path that eventually led to the founding of one of the world's largest liquor empires. But maybe it was fate—in Yiddish, the word "bronfen" means "liquor."

Opportunity Knocks Again and Again

By 1904, Abe Bronfman had bought the family's second hotel in the southeast Saskatchewan railway town of Yorkton. It was the Balmoral Hotel's bar (conveniently located just across the street from the CPR's busy express offices), not its 60 rooms, that captured the Bronfmans' interest. Within two years, Harry was in Yorkton helping Abe run it. By 1910, Abe had moved to the Lake Superior town of Port Arthur and purchased the four-storey, 110-room Mariaggi Hotel, "with telephones and an elevator that runs to every floor." That was all very nice, but its bar profits were nicer. Three years later, Sam recalled, he bought Winnipeg's Bell Hotel "with $190,000 in family money and loans," although it was likely that Ekiel put together the deal with older sons Abe and Harry and gave it to the 21-year-old Sam to run. Meanwhile, Harry had purchased three more hotels (a Yorkton competitor and two others in neighbouring small towns), purchased the lots around the Balmoral, built a dozen businesses on them and bought out Yorkton's City Garage and turned it into an automobile dealership.

However, the Bronfmans' days as hotel magnates were almost done. Many of the habitual hotel drinkers were hunkered down in the trenches on the Somme. Besides, the heady boom years were over. When economic hard times hit Yorkton, Harry still owed the Bank of British North America $100,000 in outstanding loans. Like everyone else, the Bronfman boys knew prohibition was only weeks away, but unlike most hoteliers, they decided to take advantage of it. Harry rented out his properties and left for Winnipeg to help Sam at the Bell. While there, the boys and their aging father discussed what they might do next.

Mail-Order Moguls

The Bronfmans' real business wasn't filling hotel rooms, it was filling glasses. New prohibition laws in Manitoba, Saskatchewan and Ontario made that illegal, but federal laws still allowed interprovincial liquor traffic. The three hotel owners decided to remake themselves into bottle-shippers. Their attention shifted to a town tucked away in Lake of the Woods wilderness. After all, sleepy little Kenora, Ontario, lay not much more than 100 miles east of big-city Winnipeg, which by now was full of very thirsty men.

In a bygone era, Kenora had been called Rat Portage and been home to rowdies selling rotgut to railway navvies. Once Manitoba prohibition began, Kenora exploded almost overnight and began reliving some of its unsavoury history. Unemployed Winnipeg bartenders became liquor sales-men, taking orders on behalf of Kenora's new mail-order merchants. Winnipeg newspapers reaped an advertising windfall, as many of those merchants placed hundreds of lines of advertising to promote their brands and services.

Abe quickly shut down the Mariaggi and headed to Kenora, where he opened a mail-order house to supply "the 'Peg." Once the Kenora operation was up and running, he boarded a train to Quebec and soon had a Montreal outlet ready to quench the thirst of eastern Ontario residents.

By the end of 1917, a federal government order-in-council had plugged the mail-order loophole, and it looked like the Bronfman's nascent bottle-shipping business was dead. But it took sedate-paced Ottawa until early 1919 to pass the act banning interprovincial shipments, and passage came with a catch. Before cross-border shipping was outlawed, the Senate required each province to hold a plebiscite to ensure the measure had the citizens' blessing. For some reason, the federal government set the plebiscite dates far in the future: October 1920. For more than a year, interprovincial liquor shipments would continue to be legal.

In the meantime, Harry had moved back to Yorkton and opened the Canada Pure Drug Company, which appeared to be a supply business tapping the "medicinal purposes" liquor trade. Holding a provincial licence allowed the company to apply for a federal bonded-warehouse licence. Harry wasted no time. While Liberal friends in Ottawa went to work helping him obtain that licence, back in Yorkton, a hastily assembled construction crew built a warehouse next to the Balmoral Hotel. Soon they were building another. Locals were puzzled. What on earth were they going to put in these empty structures? Soon residents in nearby towns scratched their heads, too, as Bronfman warehouses appeared in Bienfait, Gainsborough, Oxbow, Estevan, Carnduff and other Saskatchewan border towns. New locks were screwed into doors of old sheds; new iron bars were installed on windows of vacant stores. During that crazy bottle-shipping bonanza, over 60 mail-order businesses did a roaring trade in Saskatchewan alone, and others in Alberta and British Columbia had as many orders as they could handle.

Once a company held both a provincial operating licence and a federal bonded-liquor licence, it could import whisky into Canada. All the head-scratching in Yorkton stopped once railcars started to clatter onto the siding. Even before saws rasped and hammers thudded, the Bronfmans had placed significant orders at world-renowned Scottish distilleries. Those orders began to arrive in December 1919, each boxcar crammed with 1,600 cases of whisky and every case containing 12 bottles of smooth, aged Highland ambrosia.

When the initial five cars rolled into Yorkton on Christmas Day—a wonderful present for the parched people of western Canada—the sight was enough to make the conscience-stricken Yorkton customs officer ring up his Regina superior for advice. Bronfman's shoddily built warehouse will collapse under the weight of it all, he protested. What should I do? Regina's answer was clear: shut up and release the whisky. Then another 27 cars of Scotch were shunted onto the siding. Harry and Sam worked around the clock to empty them all. They had customers waiting.

There were no banks of offices inside the warehouses, no tables holding rows of telephones, no shifts of dozens of order-takers. The Bronfmans weren't filling orders one bottle at a time. As the plebiscite dates moved inexorably closer, their objective was to move as many cases—as many boxcars full of cases—as they could, as fast as they could. Volume sales were the key to quick riches.

While some individuals figured into deliveries from

Bronfman warehouses (Winnipeg's police chief purchased his Scotch by the case, and the Bronfman boys' lawyer ordered up 7 cases of wine, 6 cases of brandy, 5 cases of Scotch, 10 cases of gin, 2 cases of liqueurs and a case of rum), preferred customers were other mail-order houses and large retail outlets such as the Hudson's Bay Company. The Bay's Calgary store once took a single delivery of 500 cases of rum, 300 cases of Scotch and 20 cases of brandy, presumably to fill phone orders from Saskatchewan.

Those wood-framed structures stacked to the rafters with liquor were much more than mere warehouses. Soon there was a name to distinguish them from typical storage facilities. Nobody knew who first uttered the term, but before long everyone knew what a man was talking about when he mentioned a "boozorium." And when it came to naming Saskatchewan's boozorium king, the crown belonged to Harry Bronfman—and he knew it. "With the exception of two small concerns in Saskatoon which have practically run out of stock," he told the *Winnipeg Tribune*, "the liquor business . . . is controlled by me." The Bronfman boozoriums might have seemed out of place, located as they were in tiny towns far from large metropolitan centres, but their proximity to the Canada-US border would soon open the doors to profits that would make the Bronfmans' mail-order bonanza appear trivial.

CHAPTER

Cashing in on the "Other" Prohibition

THE PLACE WAS PACKED; estimates varied from 8,000 to 10,000. people This wasn't Podunk, Iowa, it was Boston, Massachusetts. Row upon row they sat, staring up at the stage in anxious anticipation. The noise would have been louder in that cavernous auditorium (dubbed a "tabernacle" on this particular Sunday) but for the sawdust that muffled hundreds of shuffling feet. The crowd's applause acknowledging the choir's spirited performance turned suddenly thunderous. "Look, there he is!"

Striding confidently across the stage, his face wreathed in a smile of welcome, arms outstretched as if he might take the entire cheering throng into his embrace, was the man they'd waited to see and hear. Legs braced, he stood on the lip of the stage, pivoting this way and that. This was Billy Sunday, the 20-year phenomenon of the evangelical "sawdust trail." That night, as on many other nights, he brought a message that would resonate in the hearts of thousands sitting before him. "I am the sworn, eternal and uncompromising enemy of the liquor traffic," Sunday shouted. "I have been and will go on fighting that damnable, dirty, rotten business with all the power at my command."

Sunday sprinted across the stage, arms flailing, fist punching the air, foot stomping the boards, emphasizing words that carried to the farthest corners of the auditorium. "It is my opinion that the saloonkeeper is worse than a thief and a murderer. The ordinary thief steals only your money, but the saloonkeeper steals your honour and your character. The ordinary murderer takes your life, but the saloonkeeper murders your soul."

Voices murmured assent, and Sunday whirled at the sound, bending low, pointing down at the audience. "The saloon is a liar! It promises health and causes disease. It promises prosperity and sends adversity. It promises happiness and sends misery." Heads nodded and murmurs turned to applause, propelling Sunday across the stage on his knees, as if sliding for home plate, which he had done as the base-stealing wonder of the Chicago White Stockings and Philadelphia Phillies before he found Jesus and millions found in Sunday a voice of reason, a voice of faith, a voice of hope.

Sunday's words tumbled from his lips, mesmerizing the

crowd. "I tell you that the curse of God Almighty is on the saloon. Legislatures are legislating against it. Decent society is barring it out. The fraternal brotherhoods are knocking it out. The Masons and Odd Fellows and the Knights of Pythias and the A.O.U.W. are closing their doors to the whiskey sellers . . . It is headed for hell; and by the grace of God, I am going to give it a push with a whoop."

The auditorium rocked with laughter and cheers. Sunday knew the time was right. "Say, will you line up for the prohibition?" he challenged. "Men of Boston, Massachusetts and our nation, how many of you will promise that by the help of God you will vote against [liquor]? Stand up! Let me have a look at you!" A multitude rose in response.

Big-Time Booze Business

About the time the Canadian prairies were holding prohibition plebiscites, two-thirds of American states had already outlawed booze. By then, it was obvious to most Canadians—and the Bronfmans—what was likely to transpire. It was no accident that the Bronfmans' boozoriums were not located in major Canadian centres. Not even Montreal or Toronto could compare to the huge potential markets serviced by an army of American bootleggers.

Many Canadians were unaware that America's prohibition struggles went back at least a century. History didn't matter to Harry, Sam and Abe. What mattered was that Prohibition would soon be federal law. In 1918, the Eighteenth

Amendment to the US Constitution had begun its journey through state legislatures. Just one year later, the last state legislature to vote—Nebraska's—adopted the amendment unanimously. With that, it became final. On January 16, 1920, Prohibition would be proclaimed law throughout the United States.

The Bronfmans moved quickly. Inside American warehouses sat millions of dollars' worth of liquor, destined to be poured down the drains. By US Prohibition's first anniversary, the Bronfmans had bought up 300,000 gallons of liquor from grateful American distillers and had started to ship it south again through rum-runners and their bootlegger buddies. This required a US sales representative, and they found the perfect man for the job. Former Winnipeg bartender Harry Sokol was an enterprising man who had built what amounted to the first Canada-US pipeline. Sokol poured thousands of gallons of good Canadian whisky into a pipe that ran between two cattle barns, one in Emerson, Manitoba, and the other across the border. That was the kind of moxie the Bronfman boys appreciated. They located Sokol living a bachelor's life in the CPR's Royal Alexandria hotel in Winnipeg, where, according to future sportswriter Jim Coleman (who lived in the same hotel as a youngster), Sokol had "astonishingly attractive young ladies whom he introduced to me as his 'nieces.'"

Sokol shook hands with Sam and headed across the border to meet with bootleggers, negotiating prices and organizing deliveries. The Bronfmans wanted exclusive deals, and they got them. Americans liked the Bronfman benefits. The brothers were aggressive, well-organized merchandisers who already had a string of easy-to-reach warehouses full of what thirsty Yanks could not do without. The Bronfmans also guaranteed delivery; if Canadian officials seized those goods before they crossed the border, the Bronfmans would replace the confiscated merchandise at no cost to the buyer. Armed with sales ammunition of this heavy calibre, Sokol targeted savvy bootleggers, scoring hit after hit.

By 1922, Sokol was living in a sprawling Regina residence. While appearing to enjoy the high life of a super salesman, Sokol, in some ways, was a controlled and disciplined man. He didn't smoke and—tellingly—never drank.

Harry Bronfman had long ago given up his Yorkton car dealership, but not its premises. The City Garage became a different kind of profit centre. After a car full of whisky leased to his Trans-Canada Transportation Company was seized by the Saskatchewan Liquor Commission, Harry stopped transporting the goods. He adopted the same "U-pickup" strategy used by rural bootleggers in Manitoba and Alberta and simply waited for American rum-runners to drive the back roads to collect the booze themselves. At the very least, the policy kept Bronfman drivers from absconding with either Harry's booze or the bootlegger's money.

The Yorkton garage offered visiting American "businessmen" a convenient automotive repair and maintenance service. The showroom displayed used cars, which Harry sold "as is" (meaning loaded with booze) to farmers who might be interested in engaging in a little free-enterprise activity. It was an enticing proposition: the rum-runner's risk was minimal, the money was unbelievable and the work was a holiday compared to back-breaking farm labour. Meanwhile, the boozoriums continued to sell straight liquor to processors who concocted prescription mixtures for the drugstore trade, just as the Bronfmans' Canada Pure Drug Company had originally been set up to do.

The Bronfman modus operandi was no secret; anyone else on the Canadian side could have done the same. There was nothing illegal about exporting alcohol to Americans, providing the paperwork indicated that the export's destination was south of the US (usually Mexico). Where the booze went after it crossed the border was not Harry's responsibility. The Canadian government became an eager wink-and-nudge accomplice. With bottled alcohol worth $23 million changing hands at the border in 1920 alone, even the most obtuse Ottawa bureaucrat recognized the bottom-line advantage Canada's validation tax provided. It was, as the *Financial Post* succinctly put it, "a tidy bit towards Canada's favourable balance of trade."

The New "Distilleries"

In western Canada, only the Bronfmans had, in modern parlance, the positioning to make good on promises and the

ability to connect with US "dealers" of potentially significant size. Others tried. Southeast Saskatchewan's Sair family
had been successful farmers. Like the Bronfmans, the Sairs
had fled Russia, and like Ekiel, the elder Sair had made a
significant income through horses, building a huge barn in
Estevan. Sons Isaac and Jacob invested in real estate. Their
timing was bad; the pre-war boom collapsed, and Estevan
and Moose Jaw real-estate values plummeted. Watching
the Bronfmans supply the new mail-order houses, the Sairs
decided to become bottle-shippers, too, opening outlets in
Gainsborough, Glen Ewen and Oxbow. When the US went
dry, Isaac went across the border to drum up business and
even supplied guides to help rum-runners get quickly and
safely to and from their warehouses. But the Sairs became
dissatisfied with merely retailing Bronfman booze and
decided to manufacture their own product.

Instead of taking the time to distill alcohol from grain
mash, Jacob and Isaac bought tons of ordinary rubbing
alcohol from a Minneapolis undertaker at about a dollar
a gallon. Smuggling this embalming fluid mainstay onto
their farms in five-gallon cans was easy since the border was
less than a 20-minute drive away. The boys ran the alcohol
through the still, removed the denaturant and turned it
into whisky. However, the clever Sairs were naive about the
nature of their new business. Hijackers stole their cars, and
their customers paid them in counterfeit money and forged
cheques. Reluctantly, they went back to farming.

Concluding that anything the Sairs could do, he could do better, Harry Bronfman turned his Yorkton boozorium into a distillery. Overproof ethyl alcohol purchased from Kentucky and Ontario distillers, real Scotch and a dash of burnt sugar for colouring was dumped into 1,000-gallon redwood vats. Sulphuric acid was also added; it ate away the oak lining of the 10 vats to complete the "aging process." Harry was in a hurry and didn't want to wait 5 or 10 years to age his product. He decided an entire 24 hours was long enough. The day after initial mixing, the Bronfmans' bottle machine poured the "whisky" into bottles at the rate of 1,000 per hour while another machine glued on labels.

The names on those labels often included the words "Highland," "Irish" and "Glasgow," giving the buyer the impression the contents had originated overseas. Some six years later, during the Royal Commission on Customs and Excise, officials reported that "in most cases these names of firms were fictitious . . . labelling was done for the sole purpose of misleading the customers." But taxmen shrugged off the issue, as "the limitations respecting prosecutions for such offences would bar convictions."

Profit margins were staggering. A gallon of ingredients worth $5.25 sloshing inside one of Yorkton's vats was worth $25 a gallon in the US. The plant (a much more accurate term than "distillery") processed an average of 5,000 gallons per week. By 1922, the *Winnipeg Tribune* pegged the Bronfmans' profits at $391,000 a month. Taxmen came calling. In the end, Sam and Harry agreed to pay a paltry $550 income tax for 1918, $7,644 for 1919 and $113,694 for 1920. When set against 1921's profit of $4.6 million, the taxes represented little more than a modest business expense.

When plebiscites affirmed national prohibition in 1920, the mail-order houses closed. On June 1, 1922, an amendment to the Saskatchewan Temperance Act restricted liquor export houses to cities of 10,000 or more. Border-town boozoriums were abandoned. It didn't matter; by then, the Bronfmans had entered into a troublesome partnership with rough-and-tumble Regina booze merchants, one of whom had jumped $15,000 bail on a Minneapolis manslaughter charge after a trucker was killed in a liquor hijacking. The men established Dominion Distributors, and manufacturing continued in the Queen City. The Bronfmans shipped the booze via railway express to offices in border towns for convenient pickup by American bootleggers.

With interprovincial bottle traffic a memory, the Bronfmans and their partners set about to quench Regina's thirst. Lou Kushner, former employee at the Yorkton plant, remembered the illicit booze business was an open secret, "something everybody did, and nobody tried particularly to hide it." The driveway that led up to Harry Sokol's well-appointed home ended at a spacious garage. Inside the garage sat large LaSalle touring cars full of booze. As Kushner put it, "This town [Regina] was booming as long as the Bronfmans were around."

CHAPTER

9

The Bronfman-Knowles
Whisky Wars

IN THE LATE AFTERNOON OF November 8, 1920, novice Department of Customs and Excise officer Cyril Knowles and RCMP constable A.G. Pyper were bumping along a road near the Manitoba-Minnesota border searching for shoe and cigarette smugglers. Allowed to operate unchecked, American smugglers would cost Canadian businesses thousands of dollars and many Canadian workers their jobs.

Knowles's duties usually kept him in the Port of Winnipeg, but occasionally the customs man did "fieldwork," and within months he had built a network of contacts and informants. That night, Knowles and his Mountie companion discovered much more than shoes or ciggies.

What transpired had both immediate and long-term consequences that Cyril Knowles never could have imagined.

The "Proposition"

As Knowles coasted to the shoulder of the road, he and Pyper could see the fast-moving silhouettes of three big cars on the horizon, speeding south toward the border. Knowles gunned his engine, eager to intercept what both men suspected to be a smugglers' convoy. They were correct, but the dozens of cases of liquor they found left them wide-eyed. Here was a problem, and the officers knew it. In Manitoba, liquor enforcement and seizure was the responsibility of the provincial liquor police, not Customs and Excise or the Mounties. However, if that fact gave Knowles pause, it was only a momentary one.

Some quick questions fired at the three nervous drivers—unemployed house painters from St. Paul, Minnesota—revealed they had crossed the border the previous night without reporting their entry into Canada. They had no visitors' visas. The officers then discovered just how lucky they were: the three rum-runners had become lost and thought they were still in Saskatchewan, where they'd loaded up the booze. The Americans were told they could be thrown in jail unless they paid double duty on their cars, amounting to over $3,000. They didn't have the cash but had been told what to do if apprehended. They demanded to be taken to one Mr. Max Heppner. As the manager of Harry Bronfman's

Gainsborough boozorium, Heppner had guaranteed their safe conduct to the border. Get back in your cars, Knowles told them, we'll follow you there.

At the Gainsborough warehouse, Knowles and Pyper not only met with Heppner, but with Harry Bronfman, whom Heppner had called in. Harry ordered Heppner to pull the cash from the safe to pay the duty. As Knowles opened his receipt book, Harry casually suggested he make the duty out for "a thousand dollars, twelve hundred or whatever amount he thought he could get away with," hinting Knowles could pocket the difference himself. Bronfman then offered Knowles a proposition, promising $3,000 extra if Knowles could guarantee that the customs people would simply ignore his operation in the future.

"Now you've got your money," Harry shrugged, "see that these fellows get their liquor and their car back. Don't you allow anything else to happen to them. They've had a bad knock."

Knowles stared at Bronfman in disbelief, then snapped his receipt book shut. "They can't have the liquor. It's seized," he told Bronfman. "They were in Manitoba, and that liquor's going to be turned over to the Manitoba government."

"What?" Bronfman shouted. "You mean to tell me you're gonna take that liquor away from these men?"

Knowles shrugged, "Why not? It belongs to the Manitoba government."

Bronfman was apoplectic, and the reason might well

have gone beyond the loss of the liquor. It is possible he understood that customs man Knowles had no right to demand anything; Knowles had overstepped his authority. "You're no man at all," the enraged Bronfman screamed. "No man I know would do a thing like that!"

Stung, Knowles shot back, "I'm as good a man as you are."

Bronfman smiled inwardly; he had found the chink in the armour of the young, over-confident customs man. "I'm not getting mixed up with the law," Bronfman said. "If you'll take off that badge and come outside with me, man to man and stand up to me for ten minutes, I'll give you *twice* as much money." He pointed at the pile of bank notes Heppner had extracted from the safe. Harry knew full well that even if he failed to beat Knowles physically, he would beat him ethically. The moment Knowles took off his badge, Harry would have a troublesome government man in his pocket, and that was worth a bloody nose or black eye.

Knowles had more to gain with his superiors in Winnipeg by staying calm than by beating up a bootlegger, so he didn't rise to the bait. Instead, he demanded the fine in full—freeing up the Americans' cars—and then had the booze driven back to Winnipeg.

For Cyril Knowles, the seizure of Bronfman whisky was both good and bad news. In spite of stepping over jurisdictional boundaries, the ambitious civil servant received a pay raise. Unfortunately for Knowles, the raise lifted him above the income level at which customs men were paid a bonus for confiscating smuggled goods. Knowles lost more money than he made. However, he also did something that eventually enraged the distilling bootlegger even further. Knowles made detailed notes about receiving Bronfman's bribery proposition.

The White Cadillac

Not long after, Cyril Knowles was again cruising rural border roads when he saw a spotless white Cadillac that looked decidedly out of place. Knowles and his partner gave chase. When the Caddie abruptly pulled over and the driver made for the concealing trees, the agents' car screeched to a halt and they jumped out. *Crack!* The men ducked for cover as a bullet whistled overhead. Knowles wasn't about to stumble around in the twilight looking for the trigger-happy driver. Instead, he got into the Cadillac, his partner got into their car and they drove back to Winnipeg.

The white car was an eye-catcher, and Knowles drove it around the city hoping someone would recognize it. Before long, someone did—Harry Bronfman, who knew the car belonged to Harry Sokol. Bronfman wasn't about to give Knowles a tip about the owner. Instead, he rang up his Ottawa contacts. Soon afterward, one of Knowles's superiors asked him for the car keys and issued him a formal reprimand for driving a seized vehicle for personal use. Incensed, Knowles asked to be allowed to state his side of the story—and more. Go ahead, he was told.

"While I am pleased to have this opportunity of stating the above facts, I regret this explanation was required," Knowles concluded in his report. "I have been alternately threatened and cajoled during my investigations by parties in the smuggling traffic. Efforts have been made to bribe me, and an attempt was made to bribe my brother to get me to leave certain territory uncovered," he went on. "My apartment has been burgled and documents stolen and everything possible done to embarrass the progress of investigations. If complaint has been made in the Sokol car case it is but another effort to hamper the cleaning up of the illicit drug and liquor smuggling traffic under investigation."

Knowles's eye-popping revelations were duly filed and forgotten.

The Fix is In—Again

Late in 1922, Knowles and three Mounties burst into Dominion Distributors. Sadly for them, their raid was made during one of the operation's few inactive periods—nobody was distilling anything—but officers found extensive compounding equipment ("compounding" diluted a brand with water and other substances). In a junkyard next door, they discovered a strip of 15,000 counterfeit US revenue stamps and forged American rum and whisky labels. Harry Bronfman watched Knowles pack all the evidence into a carton and place his official seal on the box in preparation for shipment to Ottawa.

Then, in an inexcusable lapse of judgement tantamount to putting the fox in the henhouse, Knowles accepted Harry Bronfman's offer to deliver it to the CP Express office on his behalf! Not surprisingly, when the parcel arrived in the nation's capital, much of the evidence was missing. For Cyril Knowles, matters then went from bad to worse.

When Harry told his brothers about the raid, the Bronfmans used their Liberal connections to arrange a meeting with the Honourable Jacques Bureau, minister of Customs. Knowles was in Ottawa to meet Bureau, too, with a complete list of all the evidence, but while the humiliated customs agent fumed in Bureau's reception chamber, two Bronfman brothers were invited into his office. Sam was accompanied by Allan, the sixth and youngest brother, now deemed old enough and, holding a law degree, wise enough to be part of the family business. The pair complained about Knowles's "complete lack of respect for private property." What really mattered, however, was that the bootlegging Bronfmans had managed to wheedle their way into the minister's office in the first place. When Knowles finally met Bureau, the minister immediately put him on the defensive.

"Do you have any spite against the Bronfman organization?" Bureau asked. No, Knowles said, even though Bronfman had attempted to bribe him. He told Bureau it was his considered opinion that the Bronfmans had close ties to American bootleggers. But none of that mattered. The customs agent soon realized—just as Calgary magistrate Jeremiah Travis had realized over 40 years before—that the political fix was in and he was out.

When Knowles opened the official response from Bureau's deputy minister, it contained no congratulatory remarks. Instead, Knowles read that due to his "lack of discretion and judgment" his wide-ranging activities were over. The letter went on, "Your duties are to be confined to Customs work at the Port of Winnipeg. The Department cannot authorize you to make investigations regarding Customs matters outside the Port of Winnipeg."

Still, Customs Inspector Abraham Code could not ignore leads the still-influential Knowles had been receiving through informants. Thanks to these inside tips, a huge raid was staged at the farm of Isaac Sair's brother-in-law, where agents uncovered two stills and a smuggled automobile. Inside two secret rooms at Isaac's home, they discovered notebooks detailing US transactions involving not only whisky but also smuggled watches and other merchandise. Knowles himself opened up a trunk containing neighbours' IOUs for American watches purchased from the Sairs.

Knowles's chief, W.F. Wilson, immediately wrote Knowles a congratulatory "job well done" letter. For Cyril Knowles, vindication was sweet but short-lived. Three days later, he received a telegram ordering him to drop the investigation because of the manner in which the raid had been conducted. Taking their lead from the Bronfmans, the Sair brothers had complained to their own Ottawa connection, a senator from Saskatchewan.

Three years later, the travelling Royal Commission on Customs and Excise produced thousands of pages of verbatim testimony on the evils of smuggling and corruption within the Customs and Excise Department. Commissioners listened as Cyril Knowles told his stories. By then, the Bronfman brothers were confident they had put their shadowy past behind them. Imagine millionaire Harry Bronfman's shock that autumn night in 1929 when RCMP officers ushered into his Montreal mansion handed him an arrest warrant. One of the charges was attempting to bribe a customs official by the name of Cyril Knowles. Had he been found guilty on all charges brought against him, Bronfman could have mouldered in prison for up to 11 long years. That didn't happen. After enduring the embarrassment of being handcuffed and fingerprinted, as well as short confinements in both Regina and Ottawa jails, Bronfman was set free on technicalities.

Knowles, of course, also remained a free man, in a manner of speaking. However, he lived in a paper-pusher prison, confined to the drudgery of his Winnipeg desk job. It turned out to be a life sentence; he was still chained to his desk at his death in 1932.

CHAPTER

10

Robbery and Murder

THANKS TO HARRY SOKOL'S initial salesmanship, a cavalcade of Montana, North Dakota and Colorado rum-runners began crossing the border, headed for Saskatchewan boozoriums. At first, the rum-runners were apprehensive. Canada was a foreign country. The roads were unfamiliar and most driving was done at night. An obvious reason for after-dark travel was the cars themselves.

These were heavily built seven-passenger automobiles with powerful six-cylinder engines purring under their hoods. The names McLaughlin Buick, Studebaker, Packard and Hudson were displayed on radiators and rear fenders, but these vehicles were soon universally known as "whisky sixes." At a time when most people didn't own cars of any description, anybody wheeling a Hudson Super Six down a country road might as well have bolted a two-sided sign on the roof proclaiming "American Rumrunner."

One look inside a Packard or Hudson ready for the return trip across the border would have confirmed its purpose. The back seat had been ripped out, and the space filled with a stack of up to 40 cases of liquor. Reinforced springs and floors made especially heavy loads possible. The men inside these modified machines dressed and spoke a little differently than rural Saskatchewan folk. They were different in another way, too: they often carried revolvers and pistols strapped to their torsos. Rum-runners noted that the boozorium operators didn't wear guns, and moreover, small-town rubes were trusting souls. They also noticed boozoriums were the most secure buildings found in these tiny towns. Most doors anywhere else could be opened merely by turning the doorknob or prying the lock open with a jackknife or screwdriver, and that included doors on banks and—after Saskatchewan prohibition was repealed in 1924—the new government liquor stores.

Spin-Off Bank Business
One October night in 1920, Winkler, Manitoba, earned a dubious honour as the first victim of American bank robbers. After cutting the wires at the railway telegraph and telephone offices, the gang posted a lookout at the Union Bank and slipped inside a conveniently open window. Inside, they discovered the bank clerk asleep in a bedroom

and asked him to open the vault, but he didn't know the combination. When the thieves began placing nitroglycerine around the door hinges, the terrified clerk told them he was a First World War shell-shock (post-traumatic stress) victim. Any big boom was likely to give him a nervous breakdown. The robbers were sympathetic. "We're veterans ourselves," one explained, telling the clerk he and his buddies were robbing banks because the US government refused to pay them a bonus for winning the war. They wrapped the man's head up in a blanket to muffle the explosion and led him out the back door.

Robbers were preparing their second blast on the stubborn vault when a man who had been sleeping in the livery stable across the street woke up, strolled over and saw the lookout. When the man raced to the firehall to give an alarm, the lookout pulled his gun. His fifth shot finally scored, and the wounded citizen limped back to the livery stable. Roused by the fireworks, Winkler's part-time constable began to pull on his uniform. His panicked wife protested, "Here the town is full of bank robbers and maybe murderers and you are prepared to leave me alone in this house while you go off risking getting killed yourself! I won't have it!" The policeman went back to bed. When the second blast woke others and they ventured outside, the robbers' lookout told them all to go back to bed, too. They did. The thieves drove off with $19,000, the biggest bank robbery haul in the province's 50-year history.

The following month, North Dakota robbers pulled up at a boozorium in Tribune, Saskatchewan. Waving guns at stunned employees, the thieves made off with two carloads of merchandise. Two weeks later, four armed men knocked over a Carnduff boozorium, tied up employees and a curious onlooker and loaded their cars, sprinkling nails on the street to discourage anyone from giving chase.

A two-year crime wave rippled out from there. Several citizens watched a robbery-in-progress at the Bank of Montreal in Ceylon, Saskatchewan. Why didn't they stop it? Nobody owned a gun. After a heist at the Banque d'Hochelaga in Elie, Manitoba, bandits were caught when their hijacked taxi broke down and they ran into a ditch. Thieves then made an $8,000 haul at Moosomin, Saskatchewan. At Foremost, Alberta, they snatched $121,000 in cash and $75,000 in bonds from the Union Bank. Bandits struck Melita, Manitoba, and hit Moosomin again, absconding with $3,500. At Altona, Manitoba, they made off with $2,500.

When the Canadian Bank of Commerce at Manyberries, Alberta, was rumoured to be the next target, the APP was ready. Parking their car on the outskirts of town, bandits walked to the bank and into a hail of police gunfire. They escaped but the bank was spared. A week later, a Minneapolis car crash sent a fatally injured man to hospital, and police found his companion in the car, wounded by a gunshot. The driver confessed on his deathbed, implicating his buddy and other gang members in the aborted Manyberries heist. His last words led police to safety-deposit boxes filled with ill-gotten gains from other prairie banks.

When they had cheered their prohibition victory, the WCTU had never envisioned this potentially fatal consequence. Rum-runners and bootleggers were bad enough, but violent crime was worse. The issue wasn't merely financial loss; the lives of innocent people were being threatened. Soon, someone might find themselves in the line of fire and be killed. Many prairie people were starting to have second thoughts about voting dry.

Big Blast at Bienfait

It was after midnight, October 4, 1922, and natty, bespectacled Paul Matoff was working late at the Bienfait, Saskatchewan, express office. Harry Bronfman was now sending booze down from Regina by rail, and tonight Matoff was releasing the "freight" with money collected from rum-runners playing pool and cards nearby at White's Hotel. Matoff was pretentious and pompous, exulting in the fact that not only was he part of the Bronfman business, but he was also part of the family, having married Harry's sister Jean. Bronfman driver Jack Janpolski recalled how show-off Paul would stand on the sidewalk in front of Regina's Bank of Montreal, goading onlookers into guessing how much loot was in his deposit bag. "If you said, 'Maybe $10,000,' he'd do a little dance and shout, 'No, it's $100,000!'" It was probably no exaggeration; before Saskatchewan's revised

Temperance Act forced Harry to close it up, Matoff's boozo-rium had been taking in $500,000 a month.

While express men loaded the rum-runners' cars, Matoff was still checking the cash inside the office. Someone poked the muzzle of a 12-gauge shotgun through an open window just 10 feet away. The shotgun blast blew Matoff across the floor and straight to kingdom come. The killer snatched up the $6,000 in cash and took the time to yank a big diamond ring off his victim's finger.

A local rum-runner and an American bootlegger were tried for Paul's murder but acquitted. The motive for the fatal hit was never discovered. Was Matoff mistakenly murdered instead of Harry Bronfman? Was it revenge for Matoff's role in returning two American hijackers to Canada to go to prison? Or was it simply theft of the cash? If the Bronfmans had a theory, they kept it to themselves.

Even before Paul's murder, the Bronfman brothers had harboured second thoughts about the importance of their Saskatchewan operations. Prairie profits were a pittance compared to the enormous money being made running booze across the Detroit River, along the Great Lakes and down the east coast to the huge, thirsty markets of Boston and New York. Paul's murder and the grief of Harry's sister spurred them to action. The next year, six million bottles of booze left the French-held island of St. Pierre bound for that motley collection of stationary ships called "rum row." Thousands of those bottles belonged to the Bronfman boys.

11

The Bottle King's Big Break

FOR LETHBRIDGE BREWER FRITZ SICK, prohibition meant the easy-money years were over. It was going to take all his effort to keep his core business alive, let alone expand it. It was time to put his little two-storey Alberta Hotel in Blairmore, less than a two-hour drive west, on the block. Like other hoteliers, Sick derived most of his hotel revenue from the Alberta's bar. Loyal patronage from Blairmore and the string of nearby Crowsnest Pass mining towns had earned him profits from hard liquor as well as sales of his own beer.

Drinking was one of the few pleasures that the mostly immigrant coal miners enjoyed. Now, the drys in Alberta and nearby BC had taken that pleasure away. Whisky-drinkers were going completely without, and the weak prohibition brew wasn't quenching beer-drinkers' thirst in the same way. Sick had to wonder who was enterprising—or reckless—enough to buy a dry hotel in Blairmore. The answer came from an Italian immigrant who had made his home about an hour's drive west, in the BC coal town of Fernie.

A New Business and a New Home

Unlike other Italian immigrants who lived in Alberta's Crowsnest Pass and BC's Kootenays, Emilio Picariello hadn't come all the way from Toronto with wife Maria and family to endure 10-hour shifts in the cold, wet pits. It wasn't only the discomfort, it was also the danger. In 1914, three years after Picariello's arrival, a fiery blast rocked the Hillcrest Mine near the little town of Coleman, killing 189 men, over half of the poor devils at work at the time. Nor had he been keen to slave away above ground at the row of enormous coke ovens, an open-air hell in which each sweat-streaked man manhandled a 60-pound shovel, pulling out over 30 tons of hot coke a day and earning a dollar for each oven emptied. No, that was not for a man sporting a three-piece suit, shiny shoes and a rakishly tilted homburg. Mr. Pic, as people called him, was a businessman restlessly looking for his next opportunity.

After initially working as a branch manager for a macaroni manufacturer, Pic soon established his own confectionery and cigar business. His ice-cream company put wagons on Fernie streets and parlours in Blairmore and Trail, BC. Pic played small-town godfather, ordering hampers from local food stores to be delivered to families of hard-working men and their ever-so-grateful wives, and writing a cheque to the local theatre manager for a free Christmas movie for their little bambinos.

The year Hillcrest blew, Pic was the sales representative for a liquor wholesaler, distributing bottles throughout the pass. He purchased the emptied bottles from a variety of sources, including up to 720 dozen bottles at one time from the Attorney General's department in Edmonton, and resold at a profit. "The Bottle King" welcomed the additional income; when British Columbia and Alberta went dry, Emilio was no longer selling liquor—at least not in the same legitimate way.

With his Fernie home just a short drive from the provincial border, it was easy for Pic to legally "export" liquor from Fernie's wholesaler into Alberta, while illegally supplying local whorehouses. By 1918, Pic knew there was a much bigger, richer liquor market not too far away: the state of Montana was about to vote itself dry. The closer he could get to the border, the better. He knew Fritz Sick from his days as a liquor distributor, and it is likely that Pic heard about Sick's plan to put the Alberta Hotel up for sale sooner than most. The two shook hands; the hotel was Picariello's, along with an agreement to become agent for Sick's legal temperance beer.

As hotel owner, "Emperor" Pic's stature increased. Residents voted him a seat on town council, even though the big man's shady side was an open secret. A legitimate business, the hotel became a convenient staging area for Pic's other business enterprise: rum-running between Blairmore and the Alberta-Montana border. At first, that business was legal, too. After interprovincial liquor transportation was outlawed in 1920, Pic kept the booze moving from British Columbia through Blairmore to Montana, simply because it was the only way to get it there.

A Family Business

Picariello's 16-year-old son, Stefano (Steve), was flunking his classes at Calgary's Mount Royal College. The Italian family he was boarding with was concerned: the boy had been sneaking out at night. Who knew what he had been up to? Well, at least Stefano knew how to read and write, which was more than some Crowsnest Italianos could do. Resigned, Pic brought him home to Blairmore.

At the hotel's garage, the boy soon demonstrated an affinity for cars. Hidden away out of sight of main-street pedestrians and motorists, the garage was connected to the basement of the hotel. Pic had a crew hollow out a tunnel and adjacent alcove where sacks of bottled merchandise—much of it produced by clandestine stills—were loaded into his fleet of big cars for delivery to Montana.

Before long, Stefano was no longer content to simply wash, polish and help load cars. He pestered his papa for a chance to drive. Pic wasn't about to let Stefano make runs to

Montana, but considered allowing him to drive a decoy car on Fernie to Blairmore runs, misleading police while another car packed with the merchandise roared unmolested through the pass. What was needed was a travelling companion who could curb the boy's wilful spirit and keep him safe. Drivers were too valuable to use as babysitters, and besides, some of them were as unpredictably spirited as Stefano! Maybe a woman? Yes—not just because of her moderating influence, but because the APP boys wouldn't dare put a woman at risk. One glimpse of a woman's face in the rear window and they'd give up their chase! If they searched the car, they'd discover that the two were on a harmless little drive, carrying a brimming picnic basket to back up their alibi. Pic had just the woman in mind. Ten years before in Fernie, best man Emilio had watched proudly as she was betrothed to the man he had come to rely on more than any other.

In 1915, 25-year-old Carlo Sanfidele, who marketed the cigars hand-rolled in Pic's little factory, had married 15-year-old coalminer's daughter Filumena Costanzo. After a short, unhappy time in Pennsylvania, Florence and Charles Lassandro, as they were now known, returned to Fernie. (They had changed their names to avoid some US trouble; some sources use the spelling Lasandro or Losandro.) Pic made Charlie his Blairmore hotel manager, while Filumena waited tables, helped in the kitchen, served the rum-runners who lived in the Alberta's backrooms and later helped Maria Picariello with her brood of children.

Maria Picariello and Florence Lassandro pose in a Blairmore photographer's studio.
GLENBOW ARCHIVES NA-5309-4

By 1922, Steve was regularly sitting behind the wheel of a big McLaughlin as Florence rode in the back. Perhaps she was doing more than just enjoying picnics in the mountains during those summer "road trips." While no raving beauty, the demure, somewhat submissive young woman might have held a comfortable appeal for an inexperienced kid like Stefano. Besides, who knew how things were between Charlie and Florence in the privacy of their second-floor hotel rooms? Thankfully, there was no incident between Steve and Florence. The last thing Pic needed was a cuckolded hotel manager.

The Law Closes In

The letter addressed to new APP commissioner Willowby Bryan was refreshingly free of bureaucratic mumbo-jumbo: "I find the bootlegging element around Macleod, Barons & Stavely are pretty sore at Cpl. Hidson and Const. Jones and the first chances they get they will try to railroad them so as to get them transferred and out of the way," the writer confided. "Both of these men have got things under control and work hard and for doing their duty are Sons of B. as far as the bootleggers are concerned."

The letter was signed "H3," code name for one of the "snitches" on the APP payroll south of Calgary. As the commissioner had put it in his annual report, "Enforcing the liquor act is one of the hardest and most onerous duties we are called upon to perform. The public render very little assistance." H3 was worth the money, all right. Despite the fact that "complaints have fallen off 60% this year compared with last," evidence led the commissioner to believe there was a "very large increase" in illegal liquor trade, consumption and manufacturing. Civic-minded citizens like H3 were very valuable, indeed. Now, what was it he had to say about the Alberta Hotel? Any tips about Emilio Picariello's center of operations were of special interest, in those early days of the decade destined to be called the "Roaring Twenties."

The APP wasn't the only police force anxious to apprehend rum-runners. In Montana, state Prohibition officers stepped up efforts to confiscate the booze entering the dry state and arrest the rum-runners carrying it down the so-called Bootlegger Trail. On one infamous occasion, those rum-runners included the Emperor himself. On his way back from dropping off sacks of beer just south of the border, Pic was pulled over by US Customs agents. It was bad timing; Pic had replaced the beer with eight cases of American bootlegged whisky, and lying on the back seat was a paper bag stuffed with $3,000 in cash, his proceeds from beer sales.

Behind the wheel, Pic listened as the agent told him he was going to search the car. The rum-runner hit the gas. The quick-witted agent leaped onto the running board, reaching inside to wrench the steering wheel away. Pic clamped a hand over the officer's and sped off. Safely in Canada a few minutes later, he pulled to the side of the road and finally released the agent. "Sorry about that," Pic is reported to have said, "but I'm a Canadian citizen and there is no way I'm spending time in an American jail." The agent turned around and began the two-mile trudge back to Montana.

Word soon got around to hundreds of thirsty miners that cold, full-strength beer was waiting at the Alberta Hotel. Word reached the APP, too, and they raided the bar. An officer tipped back one particular beer tap and watched *real* stuff flow into the glass. Manager Charlie Lassandro was fined $200.

Less than two weeks after the Alberta Hotel raid, Sergeant John Nicholson led his men to the CP rail sheds. Sliding open the door of a refrigerator car, police revealed

71 barrels and 12 kegs of full-strength beer. Police were still there when Picariello arrived to inspect his goods. He left quickly, loudly protesting his innocence. Police officers knocked on his door a few days later and placed him under arrest. This time, there was no walking away.

Testifying for his boss inside Blairmore Court House, Charlie Lassandro said it was all an embarrassing mistake. What Mr. Picariello had ordered from the Fernie Brewery was simply aerated water. He and Steve unloaded 19 barrels of the stuff, and when they returned, they were shocked to discover what was left inside the car was in fact full-strength beer. They left quickly to find Picariello, who came to the siding merely to seal up the car and send it back. The judge didn't buy Lassandro's story, but let Pic off lightly with a $500 fine and court costs.

The fine slammed Pic's reputation harder than his bank account. What may have incensed him was that some of the arresting officers likely were customers who ordered booze for special occasions and celebrations. This was not the way the game was played! Pic hired well-known Calgary attorney J. McKinley Cameron to appeal the fine. Cameron argued that there was no evidence the liquor was Pic's property, nor was it actually in his possession at the time. The appeal was rejected. Nevertheless, Pic had made a public fight of it, and he admired Cameron's spirited defence. Client and attorney were destined to meet again, and when they did, the stakes would be much, much higher.

The New Hire

Fernie's police chief was unhappy. It wasn't just that he hated the town, nor that the local climate exacerbated wife Maggie's chronic rheumatism. Stephen Lawson was simply bored of the same patrols along the same streets, the same petty criminals and frivolous complaints. If only he had accepted Superintendent Bryan's offer the year before to join the Alberta provincials! Perhaps it still wasn't too late. "I have had all the City Police work that I require," he wrote to Bryan early in 1922. Should a vacancy at the APP occur, he asked, "Will you consider me for same."

After Bryan read Lawson's pencilled words on the City of Fernie letterhead, the superintendent quickly wrote two letters of his own. The first was to Lawson. Bryan was still eager to put the decorated First World War vet into an APP uniform. Compared to the calibre of many recruits, trim, moustachioed Lawson was an exceptional candidate who didn't need any training. At 42, Lawson's age exceeded regulations, but "we will overlook the age question in your case," Bryan assured him. Experience, he believed, counted more than age. Bryan then added, "I am arranging with Inspector Bavin of Lethbridge to see if he can place you at either Bellevue or Coleman, Coleman preferably as there is a good school there." Bryan knew that family man Lawson would appreciate that. Then came a detail that would have appealed to the man's sense of pride: "We will arrange for you to get measured by a tailor after you join up."

Alberta Provincial Police constable Stephen Lawson was fated to become the most celebrated victim of western prohibition. GLENBOW ARCHIVES NA-3537-1

Bryan then wrote to Ernie Bavin in Lethbridge. Lawson was the kind of man Bavin was looking for, Bryan told him, "Conscientious, honest, and energetic," but just as important, "he knows pretty nearly every bootlegger and crook running through the pass." For Bavin, that was the clincher. The year before, while the big city of Edmonton processed

14 liquor violations worth $597, the APP's little Blairmore subdistrict, inside the wet-voting southwest, generated 105 cases worth close to $13,000.

Less than three weeks later, Constable First Class Steven Lawson, wife Maggie and their four daughters moved into Coleman's APP "barracks"—a single-storey wooden cottage—just a few miles west of Blairmore.

Pic's Last Run

By September 1922, Stefano no longer played decoy on liquor runs. Pic's boy now carried the merchandise. On the afternoon of September 21, three large McLaughlins rolled out of Fernie, headed east toward the Crowsnest Pass, with Steve's car loaded with cases of booze. One of the two decoy vehicles was driven by his father, who was accompanied by his mother, perhaps pleased to see Fernie friends. The convoy's departure did not go unnoticed. An onlooker had casually sauntered away to find a telephone.

Alerted by the Fernie snitch, APP constable Stephen Lawson and Jonathan Houghton, the town's police chief and rum-runner lookout, saw the convoy roll through Coleman. Lawson ran home to call Sergeant James Scott at Blairmore.

Less than an hour later, Scott and a constable watched Pic leaning nonchalantly against his car, parked beside the Alberta Hotel. Where were the other two vehicles Lawson reported? Scott dashed around the hotel. No cars in sight! Never mind, he thought; if booze had just arrived, they would find it. Scott strode up to Picariello, waving a search warrant. Picariello's only response was simply to lean inside the car's open window and honk the horn several times. Parked unseen behind some brush, Steve heard his father's danger signal.

The two policemen stood open-mouthed as Steve's McLaughlin lurched around the corner of the hotel. The thump of Pic's car door and the engine's roar snapped them back to reality, but Pic was already moving. The policemen ran for their vehicle. In a minute, a very different kind of convoy was racing up the highway, with the police car bracketed by two suspect cars. There had been no time to unload the booze, Scott knew. Pic's car was empty, which meant the lead car—Steve's—was carrying the load—unless it was a decoy, and the booze was being unloaded this moment from that third car back in Blairmore. There was only one way to know—stop Steve. Scott thought fast, slowed at a hotel, and as Pic raced by, his constable ran inside.

At the Lawson home, the telephone jangled. In the kitchen, Maggie heard her husband's terse responses—some kind of trouble, obviously. Then she heard the slap of his boots on the floorboards and the slam of the front screen door.

Lawson found Chief Houghton watching activity at the train station. He shouted at him to get the biggest car he could find—fast. Two of Pic's cars were on their way! Grand Union Hotel owner William Bell drove a big car. As Houghton ducked inside the hotel to find Bell, Lawson saw a McLaughlin roaring toward him. The policeman stepped fearlessly into the car's path, arm raised. Pedestrians stared as the vehicle hurtled toward the uniformed man. Lawson recognized the driver—Pic's kid—a split second before he jumped aside. Enveloped in billowing dust, he pulled his revolver and fired two warning shots. Inside the McLaughlin, Steve gasped and watched blood flow.

Slowing on the road as it twisted around Crowsnest Lake, Steve tried to identify the vehicle closing on him. His father had hung well back, covering his escape. These were police. Steve stomped on the gas pedal, and the McLaughlin ate up the gravel. Staring through the windshield at the receding car, Lawson knew the chase was futile. Bell's eyes widened as he glimpsed Lawson reach for his revolver. The constable leaned out the window, aimed as carefully as dust and speed would allow. *Bam!* Useless—the shot went wide. Lawson decided to try again. As he levelled his gun, he felt the car slow. Feels like a flat, Bell mumbled morosely.

The three men were still standing at the side of the road when Pic pulled up behind them. Lawson strode over and leaned through the window. "You had better get your son back," he hissed at Pic, "because if you don't I'll go and get him!"

A few hours later, after a catch-up conversation with Lawson in Coleman, Sergeant Scott was driving back to Blairmore when he saw a car on the shoulder, driver's door open, and an arm thrust out in a signal for him to stop. Scott stopped, and Emilio Picariello strolled up.

Alberta Provincial Police sergeant James Scott searches a car during the hunt for Steve Picariello. GLENBOW ARCHIVES NA-2899-12

"You didn't get the load," Picariello chuckled. Scott informed Pic he was charging him with speeding and blocking the road, and there would be more motor vehicle charges against Steve, too. "That don't worry me," Pic shrugged. "All I care about is saving my load and it is lucky for Lawson he did not shoot my boy." But after fruitless inquiries about Stefano in BC border towns, Pic grew worried. If the boy has been shot, others heard him vow, he would "get every goddamned policeman in the 'Crow."

Back home, a shaken Emilio Picariello replaced the telephone receiver, his worst fear confirmed. Stefano *had* been shot, but "the son of a bitch" calling from Fernie didn't know if the boy was dead or alive. He paced back and forth in his crowded kitchen, making the men around the table uneasy and driving Maria to distraction. In the doorway, Florence stood biting her lip. Where was Stefano? Lying in a hospital? Sitting in the parked car bleeding to death? Pic had to know, and the one man who might know was the man who had shot him: Stephen Lawson. He would visit the cop.

"I'm coming with you," Florence said defiantly. Pic waved her off, but she was insistent. "Get your gun," he told her, stomping through the house. A few minutes earlier, Pic had made his feelings about Lawson clear to the bunch loitering out front of the hotel: "If he has shot my boy, I will kill him tonight, by God." He snugged his revolver into his coat pocket. Two of the men at the table traded looks. Pic was acting crazy, and the woman was no help. Who knew what might happen? They rose to their feet and made for a car parked behind the hotel.

12

Vengeance and Retribution

SHIRTLESS, BRACES DANGLING, LAWSON sat quietly inside his home office with Maggie and six-year-old daughter Tibby. He hunched over a new handle, wedging it into the axe head, as much for Maggie's sake as his, since she often split wood for the kitchen stove. The abortive attempt to confiscate Pic's whisky load had been frustrating. Feeding the horse after dinner and fiddling with the axe handle were physical, mindless after-dinner chores that soothed jangled nerves.

Tibby was impatient. The sooner Daddy fixed the axe, the sooner she and Mom could go to the picture show. A block and a half away at the Grand Theatre, sister Peggy, 13, was waiting with friends for the theatre to open. Loitering in the kitchen, 12-year-old Kathleen and 9-year-old Pearl had decided to visit the Plante kids across the street.

The low rhythm of a car engine made Maggie glance through the half-opened side door. A car was approaching the house. Lawson looked up at Maggie—*who?* "It's the sergeant," Maggie said. A split second later, as the vehicle rolled beneath the office's front window, Maggie changed her mind. "No, it isn't," she said. "It's a man and woman with a red tammie on." Reaching for Tibby's hand, Maggie got up, intending first to retrieve the movie tickets from the desk drawer, then take Tibby into the kitchen for a quick face-wash before they left.

A man bellowed, "Lawson!"

Lawson rose and walked into the sitting room and squinted through the front screen door. Even through the mesh he recognized Pic. Had he come to rub it in? Lawson stepped down the three wooden steps to the rock-strewn drive. "Yessir!" he sneered. Inside, Maggie found the tickets quickly and then walked into the kitchen.

At the rear of the house, Pearl and Kathleen heard a car approach and someone shout for their father. The two ran up the alley to investigate. Peeking around the corner of the house near the left rear fender of the idling car, the girls watched their daddy lift his right foot onto the running board, brace his arms against the driver's door and lean close to the open window. The two eavesdropping girls couldn't make out the conversation, but it was clear to

Florence Lassandro, sitting next to Pic. "Where's my boy?" Pic asked.

The policeman shrugged. "I don't know."

"You're going with me to get him; you shot him."

"What about it?" Lawson asked. Steve wounded? That was news! He wanted to hear more about this. But instead of explaining, Pic began to threaten.

More Gunfire

Peggy Lawson and her friend Effie Stout had been joshing with some boys at the Grand when two McLaughlins had purred slowly up Main Street, disappearing around the corner. The boys were excited: it was Pic! The name hadn't meant anything to Peggy until earlier that day.

Peggy had been at the station, watching the bustle around the train, when her dad ran up to Chief Houghton and they both dashed off. Minutes later, everybody at the station heard gunfire echo over from Main Street. By dinnertime, most of the town knew Peggy's dad had shot at Pic's son and chased him darn near to the BC border. When her dad arrived home, Peggy hovered at the office door, watching him break open his gun, shake out the cartridges and slide the weapon into the desk drawer. She was desperate to know what had happened. "I was trying to get a car to stop," he said offhandedly. Peggy waited. "It wouldn't stop."

Her father's reply wasn't enough to satisfy Peggy's curiosity. What did Pic look like? Why was her dad after his son?

What was Pic doing back in Coleman? Maybe there would be more shooting tonight! "Let's follow them up," she urged Effie. The girls ran up Main. They spotted the two big cars immediately, parked a block away on the other side of the street in front of the post office. Effie hung back, but Peggy crossed over and walked to within a few feet of the closest McLaughlin. A big man with a moustache—Pic!—was standing beside the open passenger door. He leaned down and placed something on the lap of a girl sitting inside.

"Thank you," the girl said, looking up at him. Pic mumbled something—Peggy caught the word "Crowsnest"—then watched as Pic climbed back inside. The car rolled slowly down Main. The lights on the other big car parked behind blinked on as it pulled out and followed Pic. Within seconds, Pic had turned left at the theatre corner and disappeared. Peggy and Effie began walking rapidly back to the theatre.

Back at the house, Pearl blinked in surprise as her daddy abruptly jumped up on the car's running board with both feet. Encircling the driver's neck with one arm, he reached inside the car with the other. The two men pushed and pulled, rocking the car to and fro. Stunned by the frantic movements of the adults, Pearl didn't hear her frightened sister retreat back down the alley. As her father tussled with the driver, the vehicle unexpectedly began rolling backwards toward Pearl and then—*bang!*

Jolted by a handgun's sudden explosion, Pearl screamed, whirled about and ran down the alley, crying "Mama!" Her wails were punctuated by more shots. Was someone chasing her? Twisting about, Pearl saw her daddy at the corner of the house. He stumbled and pitched forward, collapsing on the ground.

Hand on the kitchen faucet, Maggie started at the first shot. "What have you knocked over, Tibby?" she asked.

The six-year-old's voice floated through the kitchen doorway, "Nothing, Mama." Two more sharp reports rang out.

Maggie's breath caught in her throat. *Shots, at that car! Calm—be calm for the girls' sakes!* "Oh, Daddy wants to take that woman to jail and she doesn't want to go!" Maggie called out lightly, already striding through the kitchen. "I'll go and see." Another shot erupted before she reached the side door.

Shots echoed up Second Street and across Central Avenue as Peggy and Effie rounded the Grand Theatre. Just as Peggy hoped—more gunfire! Anxious to see where it was coming from, she almost collided with Chief Houghton, who was walking through town to meet with her father.

"Pic's shooting!" Peggy shouted. She followed the chief's gaze across the open lots and low one-storey buildings. Peggy saw a car that looked like Pic's bouncing through a vacant lot strewn with tin cans, headed for Main Street and—what was that lying in a heap by the corner of her house?

"Peggy, that's your daddy!" Houghton said, as if he had read her mind.

This photo recreation, taken for the murder trial, shows what Coleman resident Henry Snoad saw during the early evening of September 21, 1922. A "whisky six" (possibly one of Picariello's fleet) is parked at the front door of the Lawson residence. The Miners' Hospital is next door. GLENBOW ARCHIVES NA-4691-3

Half a block down and across the street from the Lawson home, Henry Snoad shouted to wife Nellie, "That sounds like revolver fire!" and stepped out onto his porch. He noticed a big car parked in front of the constable's house. Two more shots rang out. Henry glanced back at Nellie. "I guess they're after Lawson," he mumbled. After the ruckus earlier in the afternoon, Snoad didn't need to explain who "they" were. He walked quickly through the yard and up toward the Lawson residence.

By the time Maggie stepped down into the alley, nurse Lucy Thorpe and young Fred Cole, visiting his hospitalized mother, were kneeling over her husband. Her three girls were clustered nearby, wailing, and neighbours were gathering. Maggie rushed up, knelt in the dirt and cradled her husband's head in her hands. "Why, Daddy, you've been shot," she moaned softly.

Alerted moments later at his office across the street, Dr. Charles Scott ordered Cole and Thorpe to carry Lawson into the hospital next door. Maggie—policeman's wife through and through—did not accompany him. Instead, she telephoned Sergeant Scott in Frank. On that tragic evening, medical assistance couldn't have been closer, but it didn't matter. By the time Dr. Scott bent over his newest patient, Lawson was gone. Entering his back at the right shoulder blade, a bullet had ploughed left towards his heart and exploded his aorta.

Apprehension

By morning, Inspector Bavin had seconded APP members from as far away as Edmonton for the manhunt, along with RCMP and BCPP personnel. In addition to Chief Houghton's account, so many neighbours reportedly saw at least a fragment of the deadly incident that the fugitives' identities were no mystery. There could be no escape for Pic and Florence.

The next day, a few hours after the hefty Pic stumbled breathlessly up a slope in a vain attempt to outrun police, Florence, at least, appeared resigned to her fate. "Don't be afraid," APP's Mike Moriarity cautioned her that afternoon, when she was summoned to a female friend's front door.

"Why should I be afraid?" she told Moriarity evenly. "He'd dead and I'm alive and that's all there is to it."

Less than an hour after his apprehension, Pic and three policemen sat in the back seat of a Cadillac, ready for their trip to the Lethbridge Provincial Gaol. Behind the wheel was a Lethbridge garage owner named Rogers, who had been chauffeuring policemen here and there all day. Had helpful Mr. Rogers and Emperor Pic ever met before? Possibly. Was Rogers well known to police? Undoubtedly. The civic-minded businessman driving the murder suspect to prison also happened to be one of Lethbridge's most successful bootleggers.

Reliving the Anguish

Two days after Lawson's murder, Maggie, Peggy and Pearl gave evidence at the coroner's inquest, inside Coleman's town hall. Two weeks later, they repeated their stories at the two-day preliminary hearing, held at Coleman Opera House. By late November, all three were reliving the anguish again inside a Calgary courtroom, in one of the province's biggest murder trials. It took weeks for Pic and Florence's legal team to persuade one of the city's best-known attorneys to defend them, but when they did, Pic must have been pleased. Their team would be led by J. McKinley Cameron, his former lawyer.

The city's newspapers knew where the news value lay, and it wasn't with the hapless victim (if only Lawson had carried his loaded service revolver to Pic's car) or even the two colourful Italians facing the hangman. The focus of press and public was squarely on two of Lawson's children.

"Little Daughter of S.O. Lawson Testifies," the *Calgary Herald* informed its readers, and "13 year Old Peggy gives evidence Clearly, but Breaks Down and Sobs When Describing Tragic Scene." Peggy wasn't alone. "Scores of women . . . were palpably affected and handkerchiefs were used freely to stop the welling tears," the newspaper confided. Judge William Walsh had the courthouse corridor cleared, simply so testimony could be heard over the babbling of the mob behind the courtroom's closed doors.

"Open-and-shut" was how many pundits described the case against the pair. In fact, the six-day *The King v. Picariello and Lassandro* marathon proved to be anything but that, despite the daily attendance of Attorney General John Brownlee, a reminder to the six jury members that the Alberta government, and perhaps the public, expected convictions. To no one's surprise, McKinley Cameron allowed neither of the accused to testify.

But the victim died of *one* bullet wound, not two. One of the accused was innocent of the hanging offence. The troubling question remained: who fired the fatal shot? Sure, a .38-calibre slug killed Lawson, but who held the .38? Nobody knew. Not Pearl, who ran down the alley at the sound of the first shot and saw only the result of a later shot. Not Peggy or Chief Houghton, standing too far away to see anything clearly. Not Joseph Plante, standing in his yard across the street; Pic's McLaughlin blocked his view. Not even Josephine Emerson, standing on her veranda on the other side of the hospital, who actually watched Lawson take the bullet. Surely, in the face of potential death sentences, the lack of conclusive proof constituted reasonable doubt about the killer's identity.

Yes, but an overwrought Florence had confessed to Sergeant Scott—albeit without witnesses or written record—that she had shot Lawson "in the stomach . . . I don't think Pic fired at all because Lawson had ahold of him." Could the jury take this hearsay at face value?

If Florence confessed to protect Pic, perhaps believing that as a woman she would escape the noose, the strategy was doomed. Mister Justice Walsh solved the jury's dilemma, presumably to the great satisfaction of the Attorney General, Crown counsel and the public at large. "If they were acting in concert, then both are guilty . . . each is responsible," the judge instructed the jury. "With that view, it is immaterial who fired the shot."

"They're Guilty" the *Herald* screamed when the jury reached its verdict. McKinley Cameron immediately initiated an exhaustive appeal process, to no avail. In early May 1923, Emilio and Florence said final farewells to relatives and prepared to meet the hangman.

Emperor Pic, photographed while incarcerated as a convicted murderer. GLENBOW ARCHIVES NA-3282-1

The Noble Experiment Ends

Cooler heads reflected that Lawson's real killer was the same one who killed APP constable C.M. Paris—thrown from the running board of a fleeing bootlegger's car—within a few days of the double hanging: prohibition itself. As far back as 1920, a disillusioned Bob Edwards conceded that prohibition was, as the RNWMP had discovered, an unenforceable law that encouraged lawlessness. End it, he advised, and "place the whole [liquor] business under control of the provincial government."

That year, British Columbia "moderationists" did just that. In their first year of operation, BC liquor stores made a $1.4-million profit, an amount no provincial government could ignore. By late 1924, all three prairie provinces had repealed prohibition, opting for government controls, regulations—and revenues. It wasn't murder that ended the dry years in western Canada. It was money.

However, prohibition's repeal would not, as the moderates claimed, put an end to bootlegging. In fact, restrictive post-prohibition regulations actually encouraged the illicit practice. Throughout the prairies, new government liquor stores closed at 6 P.M. Seals on bottles had to remain unbroken until customers had returned home. In Manitoba, nobody was even allowed to walk out of a liquor store with their bottles. Purchasers waited impatiently at home for delivery that could take one or two days. Bootleggers were open for business 24-7, and didn't care if a drinker took a first snort before he waved goodbye. In 1925, Manitoba cut rewards for information on illicit stills by 50 percent. As a result, snitches stopped ratting on bootleggers. Arrests plummeted.

In the United States, citizens endured their own Prohibition, and the unparalleled lawlessness it spawned, until 1933. America's "noble experiment" allowed Canadian cross-border bootleggers and rum-runners to prosper as never before. From the island of St. Pierre, off the coast of Newfoundland, to staid, proper Victoria, on the bucolic southern tip of Vancouver Island, liquor floated, or bounced, into the United States. Accompanied by the proper paper-work declaring a prohibition-free destination (usually Mexico or some Central American country), the liquor's transport was perfectly legal. Never mind that some of the booze would be run back *into* Canada again, to provide inventory for Canuck bootleggers. Even newly established provincial liquor stores profited from Yankee misery. Government outlets in Taber, Medicine Hat and Lethbridge were besieged by thirsty American "tourists" eager for bottles of high-quality merchandise. Amendments rushed through by a hypocritical Alberta government discouraged the unseemly practice.

For western Canadian provinces, beer issues—especially the post-prohibition fight to legalize beer-by-the-glass public drinking—proved particularly vexing. Simply shutting down breweries was not an option; breweries were licensed federally, not provincially. In Manitoba, brewers supplied the new liquor stores, but also avoided the government middleman by delivering cases directly to homes at less cost to the customer—and more profit for the brewer. The province protested to Ottawa, but no action was taken. Meanwhile, Manitoba residents had to wait until 1927 before they could walk into a legal beer parlour. Until then, Winnipeggers looking to have a few walked into the lobbies of certain hotels, where they were directed to an upstairs room registered to a John Doe.

It seemed no provincial government could get liquor rules right, either while prohibition was in force, or after its citizens had repealed it.

Selected Bibliography

Atkin, Ronald. *Maintain the Right: An Early History of the North West Mounted Police.* Toronto: MacMillan Company of Canada Ltd., 1973.

Byfield, Ted, ed. *The Great War and Its Consequences.* Vol. 4, *Alberta in the 20th Century.* Edmonton: United Western Communications Ltd., 1995.

———. *Brownlee and the Triumph of Populism.* Vol. 5, *Alberta in the 20th Century.* Edmonton: United Western Communications Ltd., 1996.

Carpenter, Jock. *The Bootlegger's Bride.* Hanna, AB: Gorman & Gorman, 1993.

Cruise, David, and Alison Griffiths. *The Great Adventure: How the Mounties Conquered the West.* Toronto: Penguin Books, 1997.

Dempsey, Hugh A., ed. *The Best of Bob Edwards.* Edmonton: Hurtig Publishers, 1975.

———, ed. *The Wit and Wisdom of Bob Edwards.* Edmonton: Hurtig Publishers, 1975.

Gray, James H. *Bacchanalia Revisited: Western Canada's Boozy Skid to Social Disaster.* Saskatoon: Western Producer Prairie Books, 1982.

———. *Booze: The Impact of Whisky on the Prairie West.* Toronto: MacMillan of Canada Ltd., 1972.

———. *The Boy from Winnipeg.* Toronto: MacMillan of Canada Ltd., 1970.

———. *Talk To My Lawyer!* Edmonton: Hurtig Publishers, 1987.

MacEwan, Grant. *Eye Opener Bob: The Story of Bob Edwards.* Saskatoon: Western Producer Prairie Books, 1974.

McKinley Cameron (J.) Fonds. Glenbow Archives.

Newman, Peter C. *The Bronfman Dynasty.* Toronto: McClelland & Stewart, 1978.

Index

142

Index

About the Author

The author of 11 non-fiction books, Rich Mole is a former broadcaster, communications consultant and president of a Vancouver Island advertising agency. Rich's most recent title is *Dirty Thirties Desperadoes*, the story of the "farm-boy killers" of the Great Depression and the 1935 crime spree destined to remain the RCMP's deadliest case for 70 years.

Rich lives in Calgary, where he is currently at work on two Amazing Stories about whisky wars on the Pacific coast, which will chronicle more than a century of liquor prohibitions, bootlegging and maritime rum-running. Rich welcomes readers' comments and may be reached at ramole@telus.net.